SEEKING ALLAH, FINDING JESUS

STUDY GUIDE

SEEKING ALLAH, FINDING JESUS

A Former Muslim Shares the Evidence that
Led Him from Islam to Christianity

STUDY GUIDE

EIGHT SESSIONS

NABEEL QURESHI

WITH KEVIN AND SHERRY HARNEY

ZONDERVAN

Seeking Allah, Finding Jesus Study Guide
Copyright © 2016 by Nabeel Qureshi

This title is also available as a Zondervan ebook. Visit www.zondervan.com/ebooks.

Requests for information should be addressed to:
Zondervan, 3900 *Sparks Dr. SE,* Grand Rapids, Michigan 49546

ISBN 978-0-310-52666-7

Published in association with the literary agency of Mark Sweeney & Associates, Bonita Springs, Florida 34135.

Cover design: Silverander Communications
Cover photography: Thinkstock
Interior design: Matthew Van Zomeren and Denise Froehlich

Printed in the United States of America

HB 06.06.2024

CONTENTS

A Word from Nabeel Qureshi 7

Session 1
UNDERSTANDING MUSLIMS. 11

Session 2
TESTING THE NEW TESTAMENT .31

Session 3
COMING TO THE CRUX 59

Session 4
JESUS: MORTAL MESSIAH OR DIVINE SON OF GOD? 79

Session 5
THE CASE FOR THE GOSPEL. 99

Session 6
THE TRUTH ABOUT MUHAMMAD 119

Session 7
THE HOLINESS OF THE QURAN .137

Session 8
REACHING YOUR MUSLIM NEIGHBOR 155

Closing Words 173
Small Group Leader Helps 174

A WORD FROM NABEEL QURESHI

I AM TRULY HONORED and excited that you will be engaging in this study guide and its companion video. They are intended to complement my book, *Seeking Allah, Finding Jesus*, which I hope you have read or are reading as you go through this study. In my book, I try to take you past the stereotypes and misconceptions of Muslims by bringing you into my home and childhood, where I had loving parents who did their best to raise me according to their Islamic faith. My goal is to introduce you to the hearts of Muslims, not just their minds. Of course, the hearts and minds of devout Muslims are connected, and it is their faith that leads them to see the world the way they do. That is why I also explore the beliefs of Muslims and how those beliefs shape the practice of their lives.

There was a turning point in my life: I became best friends with David Wood, a Christian who loved Jesus and was willing to have conversations with me about Christianity and Islam. We didn't just talk about religion, though. We went to classes together; joined clubs and organizations together; spent time in each other's homes. We were real friends, and in the context of that friendship, I was able to trust what he had to say about Christianity and understand how it could be the true religion, a potential I had thought impossible before. At the same time, we investigated Islam together, and he helped me see many faults in its foundations that caused my faith in it to crumble. After years of friendship and hours of him praying for me, I finally encountered Jesus, as three dreams and a vision led me to open up the pages of the Bible, and I gave my life to Christ.

This study guide is designed to help you do what my friend David did for me. It starts by introducing you broadly to Muslims, then by helping you understand and defend Christianity, especially where Muslims tend to challenge the Christian faith. It will also equip you to understand Islam and, when the time comes, to explore the significant fault lines in Muslim beliefs with your Muslim friends. The last session is designed to give you specific tips and suggestions on how to meet new Muslim friends and show them hospitality and love.

But, as you will see in Session 1, every Muslim is a distinct, individual image bearer of God! My journey is not reproducible, and your Muslim friends may need a very different path. Consider the information in this guide as tools in your toolbox to be used as you follow the Lord's leading. In addition to those tools, this study guide will also help get you in the right frame of mind by directing you to scriptural principles, personal reflection, and the example of Jesus.

For that, I am greatly indebted to Kevin and Sherry Harney, whose names you will find on the cover of this book. They are not just random people who collated this information; they are dear friends who follow Jesus so closely that I would trust my life to them. More than once, when confronted with a dilemma, I have picked up the phone and asked Kevin for his help, and my wife has done the same with Sherry. Every time, they each pointed us to Jesus and filled us with the hope of Scripture. They are incredible people of God who understand my heart and my thoughts—and they happen to be among the best in the world at writing study guides! For these reasons, I have no doubt you will find this study guide a robust resource filled with direction for prayer, stories to contemplate, Scripture to consider, and also methods to help you remember and apply the information I teach in my videos. All to the greater glory of Jesus and for the love of our Muslim neighbors.

Once again, I am honored that you would engage this video study and excited by the potential the Lord has to work through it and through you. Jesus is amazing; there is no one like our God! People need to know about Him, and not just so they can be in heaven, but so they can have a relationship with their unconditionally loving Father here and now. So they can be filled with the Spirit and transform this world. I pray now, to the triune God of heaven and earth, that He will equip us to reach the world for their sake and for His glory. In Jesus' name, amen.

NABEEL QURESHI

OF NOTE

THE QUOTATIONS interspersed throughout this study guide are excerpted from the book *Seeking Allah, Finding Jesus* and the video study of the same name by Nabeel Qureshi. All other resources, including the reflection questions, session introductions, and between-session materials, have been written by Kevin and Sherry Harney in collaboration with Nabeel Qureshi.

Session One

UNDERSTANDING MUSLIMS

When you hear the word *Muslim*, what comes to your mind? Do you picture a very specific kind of person? To understand Muslims we must reflect on one simple and profound truth: they are people. And every person is unique. There is no one-size-fits-all description for any group of human beings, including Muslims.

INTRODUCTION

A Story of Three Friends and Three Conversions

NABEEL WAS BORN into a devout and loving Muslim home. Though he was brought up by parents who were born outside the United States, Nabeel was raised in America and breathed the air and culture of his family's new homeland. This young boy grew up in America, but he was raised to be a passionate follower of Allah.

Sherry was born into a devout and loving Christian home. Her family roots go back deep into the soil of the Netherlands. Her parents grew up in the United States in a Dutch enclave, not surprisingly called Holland, Michigan. Sherry was born and raised with all of her extended family living within the bounds of that same small city. At only five years of age, she cried out for Jesus to save her and became a faithful follower of the Savior from that day on.

Kevin was born into a loving family that showed no signs of any faith in God. His father was a computer programmer; his mother was a math and science teacher. Their home life in Orange County, California encouraged a passive intellectual agnosticism at best and occasionally antagonistic atheistic skepticism. Kevin grew into his teen years with no interest or thoughts of spiritual things.

You might wonder how these three radically different people end up teaming together to write the study guide you are using right now. The answer is both simple and highly complex. The easy answer is that all three of them became committed followers of Jesus. The complicated answer is *how* they became Christians.

Today, Nabeel, Sherry, and Kevin are dear friends and take joy in serving other Christians through their speaking and writing ministries. They are also passionate about reaching out to people who are still far from Jesus and naturally sharing the good news that has changed each of their lives.

Here is the million-dollar question: Did these three different people come to Jesus in identical ways?

You know the answer. Of course not!

Though all three were born and raised in the same country, each of them grew up in different places, different families, different religious settings, and different cultures. God placed people in each of their lives, at just the right time, to walk with them and point the way to Jesus—but each journey was unique. Nabeel, Sherry, and Kevin needed the companionship of people who got to know them, listened, loved, talked, cared, and traveled with them on their spiritual journey.

As you begin this study of *Seeking Allah, Finding Jesus*, it is essential to recognize that no two people are alike. Since this is true, then we can conclude that no two Muslims are alike. We must set aside preconceived notions, stereotypes, and the boxes we so quickly put people in. When you interact with a Muslim, at the core, you are encountering a human being made in the image of God and precious to the heart of his or her Maker. If you can come with this attitude and disposition, you will be well on your way to extending God's love to a person who could one day discover the life-transforming grace and truth of Jesus Christ.

TALK ABOUT IT

Name a family member, friend, or another person who influenced you on your journey toward Jesus, and what did this person do, say, or model that helped you see Jesus and draw closer to Him?

or

What are your impressions of Muslims right now, at the start of this study? When you hear that a person is a Muslim, what thoughts and images come to your mind? Do you think these thoughts and images are accurate, or possibly not fully representative of all Muslims?

Definitions

Salaat: The ritual prayers that Muslims recite five times a day
Wudhu: Ceremonial washing before salaat
Fajr: The first of the five daily prayers offered by Muslims
Du'aa: A prayer offered before meals
Muhammad: The prophet of Islam who received the final revelation of God and passed it on to Muslims
Muslim: One who submits
Islam: Submission

Sharia: Islamic law that guides how a Muslim should live to submit to Allah

Hadith and Sunnah: The Islamic traditions of what Muhammad said and did

Quran: The holy scriptures of Muslims

Imam: A leader of Muslims, usually referring to one who leads prayer at a mosque

Sunni and Shia: The two major branches of Islam

Shahada: The central proclamation of Islam: "There is no god but Allah, and Muhammad is His messenger"

VIDEO TEACHING NOTES

As you watch the video teaching segment for Session 1, use the following outline to record anything that stands out to you.

A day in the life of a Muslim child

_____

_____

_____

_____

> *We need to understand our friends and the people we want to*
> *share the gospel with if we are going to share it with them in*
> *a compelling way.*

Islam is not just a religion, but an identity and a way of life

> *Islam is who you are; it is your very life, your identity.*

Muslims see their faith as their identity

_____

_____

_____

_____

_____

How Muslims see Jesus and Christians

_____

_____

_____

What do Muslims believe about Christianity? Muslims believe that after Jesus was raised to heaven (and they do believe He was), the followers of Jesus slowly began to abandon His message and turned Him into a god. By doing so, they committed blasphemy. So Muslims' concept of Jesus is that he was a reformer, and that Christians today are fundamentally mistaken about what he actually came to do.

Understanding Islam and Muslims

- Submission

_____

_____

_____

_____

- The Quran and Sharia Law

_____

_____

- Not all Muslims are the same

_____

> _Around the world, there are various kinds of Muslims. Not all Muslims believe the same thing._

- Where Muslims live

_____

_____

Where are the largest Muslim populations? Most people associate Muslims with the Middle East. It is interesting to note that the nation with the most Muslims in the world is Indonesia. The second largest Muslim population is found in Pakistan; number three is India; and number four is Bangladesh. None of these are Middle Eastern countries. Only about 20 percent of Muslims come from the Middle East and North Africa.

- Varieties of worldviews and devotion to Islam

Honor/shame culture verses right/wrong culture

Passionate conversations and interactions ... don't run from them

Many Muslims are open to the gospel; be open to share it with them

Can I talk openly with a Muslim about my faith? In my home growing up, all we talked about was politics and religion. That is how Muslims generally are if they come from the East and from various other Islamic cultures. In these places, people talk about what they are passionate about, and they expect you to do the same. Christians should feel free to talk about their faith with excitement and passion because Muslims are expecting it. We can feel free to talk about politics also. The key is that we not be upset if our Muslim friends get passionate in their responses. Their zeal is actually a sign of them being engaged in what you are saying.

VIDEO REFLECTIONS AND BIBLE STUDY

1. Nabeel is very clear that his goal and desire is to equip followers of Jesus to effectively share the gospel (good news) of Jesus with Muslims in a way that they can understand, receive it, and enter into a life-saving relationship with Jesus. How do you feel about this goal, and how might God use *us* in this way?

   _____

   _____

   _____

   _____

   _____

2. If you have a friend, neighbor, or family member who is Muslim, share about your relationship with this person. What about them do you most appreciate and respect? What, if anything, have you done that has opened the door for a deeper friendship and more honest conversation about faith?

   _____

   _____

   _____

   _____

   _____

*Devout Muslims are supposed to try to follow Muhammad to
the greatest degree possible, even to such a small detail as how
they walk into the bathroom to do their ceremonial washings.*

3. What struck you as Nabeel talked about all of the prayers, thoughts of Allah, and
    spiritual reflections that happened on a daily basis before 7:00 a.m. when he was a
    little boy? What is your sense of how these practices would impact a small child?

    _____

    _____

    _____

    _____

    Take a moment to reflect on how your devotion to God is evident throughout
    your day. Think about one or two ways you connect with God naturally in the
    flow of your day.

    _____

    _____

    _____

    _____

    _____

4. Nabeel points out that most Muslims born and raised anywhere except the West
    see Islam as a part of who they are, not just something they believe. Why is it
    critical for us to understand this if we are going to reach out to Muslims and hope
    they will become followers of Jesus? If we can't realize this and respond accord-
    ingly, what kind of mistakes could we make as we seek to reach out to Muslims?

    _____

    _____

    _____

    _____

Read: Exodus 3:13–14; John 8:58–59; Hebrews 1:1–4, 8–9; Colossians 1:15–20; and Matthew 1:22–23

5. Muslims believe that Jesus is a prophet and a Messiah, but *not* God Himself. What is the problem with this belief?

_____

_____

_____

_____

_____

What do Muslims believe about prophets? According to Muslims, 124,000 messengers, called prophets, have come to this world to lead every people group to Allah. These prophets were sent by Allah, and they include people such as Adam, Noah, Moses, Abraham, Lot, Jacob, and Jesus.

6. Why is the belief that Jesus was God in human flesh essential to the Christian message and faith? If we removed this belief, what would happen to our faith? Why is it essential that Muslims come to see Jesus as God and not just a prophet?

_____

_____

_____

_____

How do the messages of Christianity and Islam differ? The essential message of Islam is that people ought to submit to Allah and follow him. In Christianity, the essential message is the problem of mankind . . . we have sinned and rebelled against God. In Islam, the essential message is that we are all ignorant and we have all gone our own ways. Muslims believe that if they are guided and told how to follow God (by sharia), then they can and will follow God.

Read: John 4:19–26; John 1:35–43; Matthew 1:1, 16–18; Matthew 16:13–20; and Matthew 26:59–68

7. The term *Messiah* means different things to different people. What do Muslims mean when they say Jesus was the Messiah? What do Christians mean when we say Jesus is the Messiah, and how does this differ from what Muslims mean? How is the Jewish vision of a coming Messiah different than what Christians believe?

_____

_____

_____

8. Nabeel says that the heart of Islam is to submit to and obey Allah. But the heart of Christianity is to repent of sin and love God. How can these beliefs lead to different visions of God and different lives?

_____

_____

_____

How do people from the East and the West see the world differently?
In the East, people tend to make decisions based on honor and shame. It doesn't really matter what you personally think is right or wrong. You should do what is socially the "right thing to do." Family, culture, and recognized authorities determine what should be done, and people tend to follow these expectations. When you do, it leads to honor. When you ignore these expectations, it leads to shame.

In the West, we tend to make decisions based on innocence and guilt. What does that mean? In the West, people tend to think in terms of right and wrong. We do what we think is right. This means if someone does something that is wrong, we tend to show compassion if we discover that they thought it was the right thing to do.

9. Tell about the home in which you were raised. Did you avoid talking about religion and politics, or was there open and vigorous conversation? Most people raised in Middle Eastern culture are very vocal, passionate, and articulate about their faith. How can this be an open door and a helpful reality for us when we want to talk about our faith? Why is it important that we not take offense if we are having a conversation with a Muslim about faith and they strongly disagree with us?

_____

_____

_____

_____

The Islamic worldview is important to understand. Basically,
the way Muslims see the world, devout Muslims, is that Allah
has created this world to worship and serve him.

10. There are many different kinds of Muslims. Why is it impossible to describe all Muslims with the broad stroke of a brush and one narrow depiction? Why is characterizing all Muslims as identical a dangerous practice and a hindrance to our sharing the gospel with them?

_____

_____

_____

_____

How many Muslims are there in the world? And how many Christians are there in the world? A Pew Forum survey indicated that in 2011, there were 2.6 million Muslims in the United States, or .8 percent of the population. That percentage is projected to grow by the year 2030 to approximately 1.7 percent, or one out of every fifty people. The global statistics are much higher. There are 1.61 billion Muslims around the world today. That is a quarter of the world's population. *(cont.)*

The 2012 Pew Forum survey showed that there are 243 million Christians in the United States, or 78 percent of the population. Globally, there are 2.2 billion Christians, which is 32 percent of the world's population.

11. Why is it important that we get to know each person we meet (Muslim or otherwise) and take time to hear his or her story? What kind of questions can we ask that will advance our conversations and friendships specifically with Muslim friends, neighbors, and acquaintances?

_____

_____

_____

_____

> *Muslims believe that Judaism slowly became corrupted, also that Christianity slowly became corrupted, and that Islam is the only incorruptible faith.*

12. How can building a friendship with a Muslim, including having spiritual conversations and learning about their journey of faith, actually deepen your Christian faith?

_____

_____

_____

_____

How might this journey drive you more into prayer, the Bible, apologetics, and your love for Jesus? What are one or two steps you can take to deepen your faith in one of the areas listed above?

_____

_____

_____

_____

CLOSING PRAYER

Take time to pray in any of the following directions:

- Ask God to help you, and the Christians you know, learn to see Muslims as people loved by God and in need of a Savior.

- Pray for fear to be removed and for affection to grow between Christians and Muslims.

- If you have people in your life who come from an Islamic background, pray for them by name and ask God to use you to shine His light and share His love with these people.

- Invite the Holy Spirit to give you the boldness to have vigorous and passionate spiritual conversations with the Muslims God brings into your life.

- Cry out to God for Christian parents and grandparents to take the spiritual training of the next generation seriously. Ask God to help them teach children and grandchildren to pray, know the Bible, love God, and walk close with Jesus.

- Pray for peace in the war-torn places of the world that are often filled with Muslim people.

How can some Muslims be so violent and others so peaceful if they all believe the same things and follow the same book? Disagreements on the body of canonical literature is what causes so many different varieties of Islam. Peaceful Islam focuses on certain parts of the hadith and the Quran that encourage love and compassion. Other Muslims, such as terrorists in the Middle East, interpret the violent parts of the hadith as the ones that take precedence and the violent sections of the Quran as the ones they ought to follow. *(Note: To a certain extent, this is no different than certain Christian groups drawing on specific passages of the Bible to justify their own idiosyncratic beliefs.)*

Session One

BETWEEN SESSIONS

PERSONAL REFLECTION

Take time in personal reflection to think about the following questions. Journal your responses if you like.

As he was investigating the Christian faith, Nabeel asked God to reveal Himself. If you are a follower of Jesus, how has God revealed Himself to you, spoken to you, and led you? If you are not yet a follower of Jesus, how might you invite God to reveal Himself in your life? What are ways you imagine God might show Himself to you as He has to other people?

_____

_____

_____

_____

_____

_____

Who walked with you as you came to know Jesus, and how did this person care for you, get to know you, and serve you along the way? How could you be more like this person?

What was unique about your journey to Jesus, and how did God show Himself to you along the way? How can your unique journey grow your compassion for those who may be traveling toward Jesus from a Muslim background?

As Nabeel looks back on his life growing up as a Muslim, he makes statements such as, "Before anything else, you represent Islam and you see yourself as a Muslim," and "Islam was my identity." Can you say the same about your Christian faith growing up ... or now? How might your faith grow deeper and more authentic if you saw your primary identity as being a Christian? What gets in the way of your having this kind of devotion and worldview? What could help you shift your thinking toward a more Jesus-centered worldview?

PERSONAL PRAYER JOURNEY

- Begin journaling your prayers for God to use you to share His love, grace, and truth with the people God places in your life, including Muslims.

- Write prayers of confession expressing the ways you have stereotyped people from a Muslim background, feared them, avoided them, and even had harsh feelings toward them (without ever having met them).

_____

_____

_____

_____

_____

_____

_____

_____

_____

What are the different sects of Islam? There are various kinds of Muslims, and not all Muslims believe the same thing. Some Muslims don't even recognize other sects as being Islam. There are two major branches of Islam: Sunni Islam, which is followed by 80–85 percent of Muslims globally, and Shia Islam, which is followed by 10–13 percent of Muslims globally. The remaining 2–5 percent of Muslims follow various other sects that don't easily fit into Sunni or Shia Islam.

PERSONAL ACTIONS

Digging Deeper into the Divinity of Jesus

Take time in the coming week to study the gospel of John and discover more about the divinity of Jesus. You may want to read the whole gospel, paying particular attention to how Jesus is referred to (and refers to Himself) in language that is reserved for God alone. Look closely at some of the following passages:

Passage: **John 1:1–18**
Insights about Jesus as "God with us"...

Passage: **John 10:22–39**
Insights about Jesus as "God with us"...

Passage: **John 14:1–11**
Insights about Jesus as "God with us"...

Passage: **John 20:19–29**
Insights about Jesus as "God with us"...

Exploring Great Resources

Nabeel tells the story about how his friend David walked with him, talked with him, debated with him, and studied with him. Love and friendship grew the relationship and became the glue that held them together. David was honest about not having all the answers, but he was willing to study, research, and discover truth in partnership with Nabeel.

Over the past years many excellent online resources have emerged that can help you grow in your faith and learn to help others walk toward Jesus. One of the best is the Ravi Zacharias website (rzim.org), where you will find helpful videos, articles, and more. Explore this site and review the resources that are just a click away.

Language Matters

Language is important. We all need to learn not only our own language but how to speak intelligently with others using words they understand. If you want to have robust and meaningful conversations with Muslims, it is helpful to have some basic knowledge of the terms they use, what they mean, and how they use them. Take time to become conversant with the simple definitions listed at the start of this session. If it helps your memory, rewrite the definitions in the space provided below.

As you talk with Muslim friends, don't assume you fully comprehend these terms, and invite them to help you deepen your understanding. Ask if you are pronouncing the words correctly and let your friends help you learn more about the words' significance.

Salaat: _____

Wudhu: _____

Fajr: _____

Du'aa: _____

Muhammad: _____

Muslim: _____

Islam: _____

Sharia: _____

Hadith and Sunnah: _____

Quran: _____

Imam: _____

Sunni and Shia: _____

Shahada: _____

DEEPER LEARNING

As you reflect on what God has been teaching you through this session, consider reading Parts 1 and 2 (chapters 1–19) of the book *Seeking Allah, Finding Jesus* by Nabeel Qureshi, if you have not done so already. In preparation for the next session, read Part 3 (chapters 20–23).

JOURNAL, REFLECTIONS, AND NOTES

TESTING THE NEW TESTAMENT

To have a meaningful conversation with a
Muslim about the Christian faith we must
understand how they view the Bible. Equally
important is that we actually understand
what we believe about the Bible. When we
test the New Testament we will discover that
it holds up as authoritative and true under the
most serious of scrutiny.

INTRODUCTION

WHAT WE BELIEVE about the Bible sets the tone for how we live our faith and how we interact with people of other faiths. If we have a solid and sensible understanding of the Bible, we will be fruitful in how we interact with others. If we have an errant understanding of the Bible, it can actually harm our ability to share our faith.

Some people think the Bible is a club we use to beat people up so we can win the religion war. They wield the Bible primarily as a weapon to prove themselves right and others wrong. The problem is that we are not called to win a religious battle; we are called to win hearts and people to Jesus. Yes, the Bible is a sword (Ephesians 6:17), but this is for battles against spiritual enemies, not our neighbors and friends who need to encounter the grace of Jesus. If we use the Bible to attack Muslims, it will be very difficult to use this same Book to show them the love and grace of God.

For others, the Bible is a collection of fairy tales and fables to comfort and inspire. Even some churchgoing folks don't take the Bible very seriously, considering it a collection of nice stories and moral lessons but not the authoritative Word of God. No serious Muslim will be moved toward Jesus if he or she is interacting with someone who claims to be a Christian but does not take the Bible seriously.

Still others see the Bible as a textbook of religious information for us to master, a set of rules and a list of lessons to be learned and followed. Such people's faith is all about adherence to a specific collection of doctrines. Though doctrine matters a great deal and following the teaching of the Bible is the call of every Christian, we must see more to the Bible if we are going to reach our Muslim neighbors.

The Bible is the Word of God, given to lead people into a real and life-changing relationship with Jesus. In the gospel of John we read these words: "But these are written that you may believe that Jesus is the Messiah, the Son of God, and that by believing you may have life in his name" (John 20:31). This declaration found near the end of John's gospel captures the heart of this book of the Bible and could be used to describe much of the whole Bible's message. When we are confident that the Bible is true and that it has been given to bring the good news of Jesus to a broken world, we can have meaningful conversations with all the people God has placed in our life … including our Muslim neighbors, friends, and acquaintances.

TALK ABOUT IT

If you were in a friendly conversation with a non-Christian and they asked you, "What do you believe about the Bible?" what would you say to them?

or

How would you respond to a person who told you, "I could never believe the Bible because it is full of mistakes and contradictions from beginning to end"?

Definitions

Testament: Covenant

Torah: The first five books of the Old Testament

Mitzvot: The 613 laws in the Torah

Injil: The book that Muslims believe Allah sent to Jesus, often considered to be the Gospels of the New Testament

Dynamic equivalency: A process of Bible translation that seeks to capture a thought-by-thought sense of the original Greek and Hebrew text and put it in language the average reader will understand

VIDEO TEACHING NOTES

As you watch the video teaching segment for Session 2, use the following outline to record anything that stands out to you.

What most Muslims believe about the Bible

_____

_____

_____

_____

How is the Bible a challenge for Muslims? The Bible is a hurdle for the average Muslim. Many Muslims have never picked up or read a Bible, and they don't really know why they believe what they believe about it. They have been told that the Bible has been changed from the original text and message. In order for Muslims to accept Christ, they have to get past this hurdle at some point. When we present the Bible to Muslims, we need to be very patient. We should not expect them to blindly accept what the Bible says. Instead, we should share historical information that will help them understand that the Bible is reliable.

How the Bible and the Quran are different in style, authorship, and the time they were written

_____

_____

_____

_____

The history of the Bible

_____

_____

_____

> *Muslims have been taught that the Bible has been changed. Even though at some point in its past it had been inspired, and that Moses gave the words of God and Jesus gave the words of God, what we have today—according to Muslims—is no longer reliable.*

The importance of covenants in the Bible

- Adam

_____

_____

- Noah

_____

_____

- Abraham

- The New Testament (Covenant)

> *The word* testament *means "covenant." So when we divide up the Bible into an Old Testament and a New Testament, what we're saying is that there were a series of covenants before Jesus and then the New Testament, which documents the arrival of Jesus, God Himself. This is a new covenant, a new promise, a new compact, a trust that God has with His people that will last eternally until the end of this world.*

What Muslims believe about the four Gospels, and what we should believe

How do the Gospels compare to the Quran in terms of when they were written? The Gospels were written in the lifetime of Jesus' disciples, meaning within fifty to sixty years of the events they record. It also means that there were still eyewitnesses living who could challenge the content of the Gospels if anything was inaccurate. Nobody disagrees with that. On the other hand, all the stories about Muhammad's life were written 150 to 250 years after Muhammad died. If Muslims can trust the stories about Muhammad's life, they should definitely be able to trust the stories from the four Gospels. These stories were recorded much closer to the actual events.

The inspiration of the Bible

Textual integrity ... has the Bible been changed?

Some ideas to help us share with confidence and humility

- Don't be offended at challenges to the Bible and questions about the foundations of your faith.
- Be humbly confident in your faith and the truth of the Bible.
- Do your homework ... know the text of the Bible but also the history of the Bible.
- Gently ask for substantiation ... this leads to a conversation more than debate.
- Get the context.
- Do research.

VIDEO REFLECTIONS AND BIBLE STUDY

1. Why is it so important that we understand what Muslims believe about the Bible in general and the New Testament in particular? From what Nabeel taught, what do you learn about how Muslims view the Bible?

_____

_____

_____

> *Generally speaking, the issue that Muslims have with the Bible is not with the whole Bible. They generally don't have issues with the Old Testament. What they have problems with is usually the New Testament.*

Read: 2 Peter 1:19–21 and 2 Timothy 3:14–17

2. Why must we be confident in the Bible and be able to defend the authority of the biblical text if we are going to have rich and meaningful conversations with our Muslim friends and neighbors? What are some possible negative consequences if we are not confident in the truth and authority of the Bible?

_____

_____

_____

_____

_____

3. The New Testament contains twenty-seven books written by different authors over many years. Why might these different authors cause suspicion and caution on the part of Muslims? How could the variety of authors over time actually add credibility and authority to the Bible?

_____

_____

_____

Why do Muslims struggle with multiple voices in the New Testament?
The Quran is one book written by one person. This means the Quran has one voice throughout the entire book. Muslims are used to reading a single author and voice. When they look at the New Testament, they see and hear multiple voices. Sometimes these multiple voices appear to say contradictory things. We know that the Bible does not contradict itself, but because the authors wrote from different vantage points and to various audiences, a casual reading can give the impression of occasional disagreement. We need to explain to Muslims that when they are reading the Bible, they are reading the work of many different people using many different voices and genres. What looks like a contradiction may simply be different voices saying the same thing.

4. Nabeel is clear that the life, death, and resurrection of Jesus is the foundation of the Christian faith. What do you believe about Jesus, and how is your faith in Jesus the unshakable foundation for all of your life? How does your faith in Jesus make your life solid and secure on a daily basis?

_____

_____

_____

_____

_____

5. Nabeel talks about how Jesus came to establish a new covenant which no longer holds people to the regulations of the law but enables them to know God personally and intimately. Why is this truth so important, and how might it be appealing to a person from a Muslim background?

_____

_____

_____

_____

_____

Read: Jeremiah 31:31–33 and Hebrews 8:7–12

6. What did Jesus believe about the inspiration of the Old Testament? If the Old Testament is inspired, and if the Old Testament is filled with prophecy of a new covenant coming, how can these truths grow our confidence (and the confidence of Muslims) that the New Testament is also inspired?

_____

_____

_____

_____

7. If Muslims believe that the original words of the Old Testament and the Gospels were inspired, how can this belief be a great starting point for our conversations about the New Testament being inspired as well?

_____

_____

_____

Now, the story of Jesus is the arrival of God Himself to lead
His people. That's what the whole New Testament is about.

8. If Muslims believe the Gospels were true and accurate in their original version, it would seem that the pressure would be on Muslims to prove that the content and doctrine of the Gospels have been substantially changed. What evidence could you offer that assures us (and could assure our Muslim neighbors) that the Gospels have not been changed in any substantial way?

_____

_____

_____

_____

9. What steps can you take in the coming weeks to strengthen your foundation of confidence in the authority and reliability of the Bible in general and the Gospels specifically?

_____

_____

_____

_____

> *It is important to know that Muslims, when it comes to the Bible,*
> *are most concerned with the four Gospels. It's because those are the*
> *four books of the Bible that talk specifically about Jesus' life.*

10. How does the existence of so many manuscripts—many of them very ancient— add authority to the idea that the Bible has not changed over time?

_____

_____

_____

_____

How does the fact that there are no serious or substantial doctrinal changes or additions in any of the manuscripts in existence help validate the truth of the Bible and God's hand protecting its truthfulness?

_____

_____

_____

11. We all know that there are many versions of the Bible available today. What would you say to a Muslim friend who claims that the variety of versions shows the Bible is inconsistent and can't be trusted?

_____

_____

_____

_____

A couple of short writings, Mark 16:9–20 and John 7:53–8:11, don't appear in the earliest manuscripts of the Gospels but show up in some of the later manuscripts. How could you explain this to a Muslim friend who says that these later additions prove that the Bible can't be trusted?

_____

_____

_____

How can we understand and explain the various versions of the Bible?

Muslims often ask why there are so many different versions of the Bible. We should point out that these are different translations of the Greek and Hebrew. It is not that there are many different versions of the ancient Greek and Hebrew; these versions are all based on reconstructions of the Greek and Hebrew text. It is the same text, expressed in different ways for different reasons. For instance, the New International Version (NIV) is a dynamic equivalency translation. The translators took the thoughts of the ancient Greek and Hebrew and translated them into English in such a way that we can really understand them. The translators of the New American Standard Bible (NASB), on the other hand, tried to translate word for word even if it doesn't make as much sense to us. These different versions are trying to bring out different things, but they translate from the same Greek and Hebrew text.

12. How might you discuss and articulate the presence of minor variations in the Bible and the historical process of writing other ancient documents, including the Quran, without becoming contentious? What are ways we can seek to substantiate our claims without being argumentative? How can we be confident and clear but also humble and gentle in these conversations?

_____

_____

_____

How should prayer factor into these conversations and relationships?

_____

_____

_____

_____

Finally, what is one action step you will take to better equip yourself to engage with your Muslim neighbors?

_____

_____

_____

_____

> *With very few exceptions, Muslims will challenge the Bible when you are talking with them. They've been taught to do that; they just believe that it is false. That's what they have been told. What we need to do is to be confident. Jesus tells us that He is the way, the truth, and the life. We can speak with gentle boldness!*

CLOSING PRAYER

Take time to pray in any of the following directions:

- Thank God for giving His Word, the Bible, to lead and guide us.
- Confess where you need to grow in your understanding of the content of the Bible and the history of the Bible.
- Ask God for discipline to study the Bible and also to dig into its history so you are equipped and ready to share your faith with confidence.
- Pray for deep and genuine humility when you talk with people who have no faith, or a commitment to another faith, including Islam.
- Invite God to bring more people into your life and sphere of influence who have a Muslim faith, or a worldview shaped by Islam.

Why are the Jews considered God's chosen people? Muslims have issues with the fact that Jews are the chosen people. We need to explain to them that the Jews are not God's favorites in the sense that God has one group who He treats better than everyone else. When the Bible says the Jews are God's chosen people, it means they have been chosen to demonstrate that God is real ... that Yahweh, the God of the Jews, is the one real God.

BETWEEN SESSIONS

PERSONAL REFLECTION

Take time in personal reflection to think about the following questions. Journal your responses if you like.

How can you be confident that the Bible is accurate, from God, and authoritative?

_____

_____

_____

_____

_____

_____

How has the Bible helped to shape your faith, and how has it been a foundation for your daily life?

_____

_____

_____

_____

_____

_____

As you prepare to share your faith with Muslim friends and acquaintances, what topics about the history and authority of the Bible do you need to study in greater depth? What resources will you use, and when will you do this study?

_____

_____

_____

_____

_____

PERSONAL PRAYER JOURNEY

- Do you pray for the people you are walking with toward a relationship with Jesus? Ask God to help you see the next steps you can take on this journey and how you can get ready to take these steps. Declare your commitment to study, learn, and become more informed about both the content and history of the Bible.

_____

_____

_____

_____

_____

_____

_____

The Bible is not the why of Christian belief; it is the what.

PERSONAL ACTIONS

Gospel Study

Read the four Gospels in the coming month. As you read, make a list of each insight you gain about Jesus and how this truth can impact your conversations with Muslims. Use the space provided on the following pages to collect your insights and thoughts; use a notebook if you need more room.

GOSPEL OF MATTHEW

Passage: _____

Insight about Jesus: _____

_____

How this could help in your conversations with Muslims:

_____

_____

Passage: _____

Insight about Jesus: _____

_____

How this could help in your conversations with Muslims:

_____

_____

Passage: _____

Insight about Jesus: _____

_____

How this could help in your conversations with Muslims:

_____

_____

Passage: _____

Insight about Jesus: _____

_____

How this could help in your conversations with Muslims:

_____

_____

Passage: _____

Insight about Jesus: _____

_____

How this could help in your conversations with Muslims:

_____

_____

Passage: _____

Insight about Jesus: _____

_____

How this could help in your conversations with Muslims:

_____

_____

Passage: _____

Insight about Jesus: _____

_____

How this could help in your conversations with Muslims:

_____

_____

Passage: _____

Insight about Jesus: _____

_____

How this could help in your conversations with Muslims:

_____

_____

How do Muslims look at the apostle Paul? The apostle Paul is somewhat of a problem for Muslims. They don't like Paul because, in their eyes, he hijacked Christianity. They think that Paul came onto the scene later and injected doctrines that made Jesus into God. In the minds of Muslims, Paul is the one who changed everything that Jesus taught.

We know that Paul was inspired by the Holy Spirit and wrote only the truth from God. But when we are conversing with Muslims about faith, we are wise to focus more on the Gospels and shy away from the New Testament books written by Paul because our Muslim friends and neighbors might be quick to ignore passages from the letters of Paul.

GOSPEL OF MARK

Passage: _____

Insight about Jesus: _____

_____

How this could help in your conversations with Muslims:

_____

_____

Passage: _____

Insight about Jesus: _____

_____

How this could help in your conversations with Muslims:

_____

_____

Passage: _____

Insight about Jesus: _____

_____

How this could help in your conversations with Muslims:

_____

_____

Passage: _____

Insight about Jesus: _____

_____

How this could help in your conversations with Muslims:

_____

_____

Passage: _____

Insight about Jesus: _____

_____

How this could help in your conversations with Muslims:

_____

_____

Passage: _____

Insight about Jesus: _____

_____

How this could help in your conversations with Muslims: _____

_____

_____

Passage: _____

Insight about Jesus: _____

_____

How this could help in your conversations with Muslims: _____

_____

_____

Passage: _____

Insight about Jesus: _____

_____

How this could help in your conversations with Muslims: _____

_____

_____

GOSPEL OF LUKE

Passage: _____

Insight about Jesus: _____

_____

How this could help in your conversations with Muslims: _____

_____

_____

Passage: _____

Insight about Jesus: _____

_____

How this could help in your conversations with Muslims: _____

_____

_____

Passage: _____

Insight about Jesus: _____

_____

How this could help in your conversations with Muslims:

_____

_____

Passage: _____

Insight about Jesus: _____

_____

How this could help in your conversations with Muslims:

_____

_____

Passage: _____

Insight about Jesus: _____

_____

How this could help in your conversations with Muslims:

_____

_____

Passage: _____

Insight about Jesus: _____

_____

How this could help in your conversations with Muslims:

_____

_____

Passage: _____

Insight about Jesus: _____

_____

How this could help in your conversations with Muslims:

_____

_____

Passage: _____

Insight about Jesus: _____

_____

How this could help in your conversations with Muslims:

_____

_____

GOSPEL OF JOHN

Passage: _____

Insight about Jesus: _____

_____

How this could help in your conversations with Muslims:

_____

_____

Passage: _____

Insight about Jesus: _____

_____

How this could help in your conversations with Muslims:

_____

_____

Passage: _____

Insight about Jesus: _____

_____

How this could help in your conversations with Muslims:

_____

_____

Passage: _____

Insight about Jesus: _____

_____

How this could help in your conversations with Muslims:

_____

_____

Passage: _____

Insight about Jesus: _____

How this could help in your conversations with Muslims:

_____

_____

Passage: _____

Insight about Jesus: _____

How this could help in your conversations with Muslims:

_____

_____

Passage: _____

Insight about Jesus: _____

How this could help in your conversations with Muslims:

_____

_____

Passage: _____

Insight about Jesus: _____

How this could help in your conversations with Muslims:

_____

_____

Study John 14–17

In John 14–17, almost all of the text is Jesus speaking to His disciples and teaching them. Read these chapters a couple of times and collect your insights on how the Holy Spirit guides the followers of Jesus and assures us of the truth and authority of the Gospels.

INSIGHTS ABOUT JESUS, THE WORK OF THE HOLY SPIRIT, AND THE AUTHORITY OF THE GOSPELS

Passage and Insight: _____

_____

_____

How this will help grow my own faith:

_____

_____

How this will help as I converse and walk with Muslims:

_____

_____

Passage and Insight: _____

_____

_____

How this will help grow my own faith:

_____

_____

How this will help as I converse and walk with Muslims:

_____

_____

Passage and Insight: _____

_____

_____

How this will help grow my own faith:

_____

_____

How this will help as I converse and walk with Muslims:

_____

_____

Passage and Insight: _____

_____

_____

How this will help grow my own faith:

_____

_____

How this will help as I converse and walk with Muslims:

_____

_____

Passage and Insight: _____

_____

_____

How this will help grow my own faith:

_____

_____

How this will help as I converse and walk with Muslims:

_____

_____

Passage and Insight: _____

_____

_____

How this will help grow my own faith:

_____

_____

How this will help as I converse and walk with Muslims:

_____

_____

Passage and Insight: _____

_____

_____

How this will help grow my own faith:

_____

_____

How this will help as I converse and walk with Muslims:

_____

_____

Passage and Insight: _____

_____

_____

How this will help grow my own faith:

_____

_____

How this will help as I converse and walk with Muslims:

_____

_____

Faith Comes by Hearing

We can learn and keep learning, and still have no impact on our Muslim friends and neighbors. At some point, we must articulate our faith, have meaningful conversations, ask good questions, and interact with confident yet humble hearts.

To prepare to begin having good conversations about your faith in general, and the Bible in particular, consider doing these four things:

1. Take time to write out three or four insights about the Bible and its authority and reliability that you learned in this session.

    - _____

    - _____

    - _____

    - _____

2. Actually practicing your ability to explain these three or four truths aloud several times can be very helpful. You can do this when you are alone, driving, taking a shower, or any time when you can talk out loud without being distracted by others. There is something powerful about hearing yourself articulate, with boldness and confidence, the reality that God's Word is true and authoritative.

3. Once you have practiced and feel you can articulate these truths about the Bible and the Gospels, practice sharing them with a trusted Christian friend. Make it clear that you are practicing in preparation to share these insights with Muslims whom God has brought into your life.

    Then humbly ask your friend to evaluate how you did. Were the ideas clear? What can you change or develop? How do they feel a Muslim might respond to this? Let your friend help shape your ability to better express these things you are learning.

    If your friend is particularly interested, you might want to direct them to the book *Seeking Allah, Finding Jesus*.

4. Pray for opportunities to share these insights with a Muslim neighbor or friend. Ask God to open doors, and invite the Holy Spirit to give you boldness as you enter these conversations.

DEEPER LEARNING

As you reflect on what God has been teaching you through this session, consider reading Part 3 (chapters 20–23) of the book *Seeking Allah, Finding Jesus* by Nabeel Qureshi, if you have not done so already. In preparation for the next session, read Part 4 (chapters 24–27).

JOURNAL, REFLECTIONS, AND NOTES

Session Three

COMING TO THE CRUX

An objective thinker who looks closely at the evidence will come to the conclusion that Jesus died by crucifixion and then rose again from the dead. If we can help our Muslim friends and neighbors discover this reality, they will take a significant step toward being able to embrace Jesus as Savior and the Lord of all history ... and their life.

INTRODUCTION

YOU ARE AT a sporting event and are excited by the play, energy, and talent of the players. You are enjoying the competition and appreciate the dedication of the athletes. The score has remained quite close for most of the game, but then it happens . . . there is a moment, a specific play, and everything changes. You can feel it in the air. You can almost taste it. You might call this a "game-changing moment!" The tide has turned; one team now has the clear advantage and goes on to victory.

A young man and woman are dating. They really seem to like each other. Things are progressing smoothly. Friends and family have given a collective thumbs-up. The sound of wedding bells might be in the air in the not-too-distant future. Then, in a matter of moments, everything shifts. A conflict erupts; words are exchanged; things are said that can't be taken back; hidden bitterness comes to the surface. In the coming weeks, the relationship unravels, and dreams of a future together are replaced with relief that the relationship is over. Though other contributing factors exist, the man and woman both track the end of their relationship to that one turning point when issues came to the surface, words cut like knives, and hearts were damaged—from their perspective, beyond repair.

Her financial world was rock solid. As a single business professional she worked hard, made great money, and invested aggressively. The bottom line kept looking better; life was good. Then the phone rang, and her world changed with one conversation. A close and trusted friend with real financial savvy had introduced her to an investment that was a sure thing, guaranteed to pay over double what she was making in more traditional and conservative investment scenarios. She had taken all of her financial eggs and confidently placed them in this one basket. The phone call was simple and short: "It turns out that the investment was a scam. I lost all my money, and so did you. I am so, so sorry!" In one moment her financial world was rocked, her trust was shattered, and her future became uncertain.

We all face times of sudden and significant shifting in the foundation of our lives. These moments can rattle us and redefine our life direction for better or for worse. This is truest when we face a turning point in our faith, when deeply held beliefs and convictions are tested.

TALK ABOUT IT

Tell about a time when you experienced a dramatic turning point in some aspect of your life. How was the landscape of your life different after that moment?

or

If a Muslim actually encounters Jesus and decides to leave their religious roots to follow Him, what are some ways the landscape of their life might change? Why is it important for us to be sensitive to this as we walk with Muslim friends learning about Jesus?

Definitions

Historical Jesus: Jesus as He can be known through historical records

Historical method: Criteria and techniques used by historians to systematically investigate the past

Criterion of multiple attestation: A principle of the historical method that posits that a recorded event is more likely to be historically accurate if it is recorded in multiple independent sources, all else being equal

Criterion of early testimony: A principle of the historical method that posits that early accounts of an event are more likely to be accurate than later accounts, all else being equal

VIDEO TEACHING NOTES

As you watch the video teaching segment for Session 3, use the following outline to record anything that stands out to you.

Discovering that history stands against Islam

_____

_____

_____

_____

Jesus died by crucifixion

* The testimony of all four Gospels

* Romans, Jews, and Christians all agree

* The brutal process of crucifixion

> *All four Gospels say that Jesus died by crucifixion. The book of Acts says it. Paul says it. Peter says it. Virtually everyone who says anything about Jesus in the New Testament mentions that He died by crucifixion.*

Muslim responses to the crucifixion and death of Jesus

* The substitution theory

* The theistic swoon theory

* The problem with these theories

> *We can be confident that history is squarely in favor of the Christian claim that Jesus died by crucifixion and that the Islamic position presented in the Quran that Jesus did not die by crucifixion poses historical problems and faith-based problems.*

The case for the resurrection

- Fact 1: Jesus died.

  _____

  _____

- Fact 2: The disciples believed He rose and appeared to them.

  _____

  _____

- Fact 3: Enemies of Jesus believed He rose and appeared to them.

  _____

  _____

What is the minimal facts theory or approach to the resurrection?
This argument was developed by a scholar named Dr. Gary Habermas and propagated by one of his protégés, Dr. Michael Licona. They argue that scholars across the board, whether atheist, agnostic, Hindu, Christian, Jewish, or Buddhist, agree on some facts about Jesus' death and resurrection. Dr. Habermas noticed that if you treat those facts as a historian generally should, you almost have to conclude that Jesus rose from the dead. What Habermas said was if historians provide the best explanations for the facts, and if they put those together into a compelling framework to say what happened, the best explanation points to the resurrection of Jesus.

How to talk about Jesus' death and the resurrection with Muslims

- Be firm in your convictions.
- Focus on what any objective observer would believe.

  _____

  _____

  _____

  _____

VIDEO REFLECTIONS AND BIBLE STUDY

1. Have you ever faced a situation where something you believed deeply came into direct conflict with the facts? How did you deal with this point of conflict and crisis?

_____

_____

_____

Read: Acts 2:22–24

2. Why do you think the death and resurrection of Jesus was such a powerful motivation for people in the early church to share their faith with others? Why does your conviction that Jesus died on the cross and rose again move you to share your faith with confidence and boldness today?

_____

_____

_____

The why of the Christian faith is the death and resurrection of Jesus.

3. The Quran teaches that Jesus was not killed or crucified. If we can gently, clearly, and convincingly help Muslims see that history clearly affirms that Jesus died on the cross, how might this impact them and open the door for deeper spiritual conversations about the Christian faith? What specific things can we talk about with Muslims that will help them see that history clearly affirms that Jesus died by crucifixion?

_____

_____

_____

Scholars who study Jesus' life are virtually unanimous that Jesus died by crucifixion. This includes Christian, agnostic, and atheist scholars.

Read: Matthew 27:22–50

4. Let's say that you are conversing with a person who suggests that Jesus survived the crucifixion—He simply passed out and later woke up and walked away from the tomb. How can you refute this as simply an impossible explanation in light of what you know about crucifixion?

_____

_____

_____

_____

What was a Roman flogging? When the Romans flogged a person, it was more brutal that most people today can comprehend. It was part of the crucifixion process that people called the "pre-death." They would tie the victim to a post and beat them with a flagrum, a whip with approximately six leather cords, each cord consisting of leather balls with shards of sheep bone and metal dumbbells. The leather balls would strike the skin, and the metal dumbbells would cause the blood vessels under the skin to dilate. Then the sheep bone would latch into the skin and rip it off. Such torture could lay bare arteries and veins and cause intestines to fall out because abdominal walls would give way. The process of flogging would kill some people before they were crucified; it was that brutal and severe.

5. If a Muslim told you that Jesus did not die on the cross because God miraculously kept him alive, or Jesus did not die because God made another person look like

Jesus (put Jesus' face on another person), how might you respond to these theories? What do these theories say about the God of Islam if he did either of these things?

_____

_____

_____

_____

> *I consider the case for Jesus' death to be the one thing that shows whether a Muslim is actually approaching the evidence historically or if he is approaching it by faith alone.*

Read: 1 Corinthians 15:12–19

6. In light of what the apostle Paul teaches in 1 Corinthians 15, what are the implications on the Christian faith (and on followers of Jesus) if Jesus did not rise from the dead? What are some of the implications if Jesus truly did die and rise again?

_____

_____

_____

_____

7. Scholar Gary Habermas came to three conclusions after studying the historical evidence for the resurrection of Jesus: (1) Jesus died by crucifixion; (2) Jesus' disciples believed with confidence that he rose from the dead; (3) the enemies of Jesus also believed he had died and rose from the grave. How do each of these realities help build a strong case for the resurrection?

_____

_____

_____

_____

Read: Matthew 26:69–75; Acts 2:14; 23–24; and Acts 3:12–20

8. Peter made a radical shift in his thinking, actions, and the words he spoke. Before Jesus went to the cross, Peter denied Him three times. Later, he boldly preached Jesus as the Savior and risen Lord. How is Peter's transformation evidence of Christ's resurrection?

_____

_____

_____

_____

Read: Acts 9:1–6; Acts 22:3–11; and Acts 26:12–23

9. Saul (later called Paul) was an enemy of the Christians and actively persecuted followers of Jesus. How does Paul's story and life transformation help build a clear and compelling case for the resurrection? If Jesus had not risen and if he had not confronted Saul, what other explanation could be given for this change in Saul's thinking and behavior?

_____

_____

_____

_____

10. Both Saul (Paul) and James were strongly resistant to the idea that Jesus was the Messiah. They had no reason to hope or imagine that Jesus would rise from the dead. How does the theory that the early followers of Jesus hallucinated His resurrection fall apart when we learn that enemies of Jesus (like Paul and James) also believed in His resurrection with such conviction that they would die for their faith in Jesus?

_____

_____

_____

_____

People generally don't die for what they know is false.

11. Another hypothesis that has been posited to explain the resurrection is that some-one stole the body of Jesus. How does this theory match up against the three conclusions presented by Gary Habermas?

_____

_____

_____

You can't effectively discuss the evidence for the crucifixion, death, and resurrection of Jesus until you are convinced of it yourself.

12. Nabeel believes the litmus test for Muslims is if they deny the death of Jesus on the cross even in the face of the overwhelming evidence. On Nabeel's journey to faith in Jesus, this test was a decisive moment. Why must we help our Muslim friends look at the evidence of history that clearly points to the fact that Jesus died on the cross? What are ways we can do this with both humility and conviction?

_____

_____

_____

_____

13. How has this session helped you build a solid and reasonable defense of your belief that Jesus really did die by crucifixion and that He actually rose from the dead? How will this defense help you articulate your faith and interact in a meaningful way with Muslims about these critical topics?

_____

_____

_____

_____

We should not seek to push Muslims to abandon Islam in one conversation.

CLOSING PRAYER

Take time to pray in any of the following directions:

- Thank Jesus for His willing sacrifice of Himself for us. All that we studied in this session about the crucifixion is not theory but actual suffering that Jesus bore to take away our sins. Thank Him for making the decision to suffer in your place for your sins.

- Give God praise for the glory of the resurrection. Acknowledge that the resurrection of Jesus is real and also the key to your salvation.

- Pray that your Muslim friends will open their minds to the history and facts surrounding the death and resurrection of Jesus.

- Ask God to give you both humility and articulate boldness as you converse with Muslims about the facts surrounding the death of Jesus.

- Cry out to God, asking Him to deepen your faith and strengthen your love for Jesus through this study and in your subsequent conversations with Muslims.

- Pray that the risen Jesus will show Himself to your Muslim neighbors and friends in powerful ways. Invite God to reveal Himself through conversations and reasonable reflection but also through dreams, visions, and any way God wants to work.

> *The Christian faith declares that Jesus physically rose from the dead. What this means for us is tremendous. We can have hope in our afterlife. Through faith in Jesus we can be assured that we will also be raised.*

Session Three

BETWEEN SESSIONS

PERSONAL REFLECTION

Take time in personal reflection to think about the following questions. Journal your responses if you like.

Are you convinced that Jesus died on the cross and that He rose again from the dead? If you have questions or struggles with this, what are they? How can you overcome these points of doubt?

_____

_____

_____

_____

_____

_____

_____

Why is the death of Jesus on the cross important and central for you both historically and theologically? Why is it critical in your interactions with Muslims?

_____

_____

_____

_____

_____

_____

What do scholars say about Jesus being crucified? Virtually every scholar (Christian, agnostic, and atheist) agrees that Jesus died by crucifixion. One scholar, Paula Fredriksen, says that this is one of the surest facts of history. But since the Quran says that Jesus was not killed nor was he crucified, Muslims have a hard time believing that Jesus died on the cross. It is important to actually get into the historical evidence here.

Why is the resurrection of Jesus important and central for you both historically and theologically? Why is it critical in your interactions with Muslims?

_____

_____

_____

_____

_____

_____

PERSONAL PRAYER JOURNEY

- Journal prayers for Muslim friends, neighbors, family members, and acquaintances. Also, pray for God to open more relational connections between you and Muslims.

_____

_____

_____

_____

_____

PERSONAL ACTIONS

The Power of Remembering

Spend time reflecting on any personal turning points in your faith journey. Identify some things that led to this shift in your life direction as well as some ways your life has changed for the better since then.

Turning Point: When I placed my faith in Jesus and began following Him

What were some of the factors that led to this turning point?

_____

_____

_____

What are some of the ways life has changed for the better since facing this turning point?

_____

_____

_____

How can understanding this specific turning point in my life inspire me as I reach out to Muslims and others who are far from God?

_____

_____

_____

Turning Point: A specific time I went deeper in my faith and experienced significant growth and connection with God

What were some of the factors that led to this turning point?

_____

_____

_____

What are some of the ways life has changed for the better since facing this turning point?

_____

_____

_____

How can understanding this specific turning point in my life inspire me as I reach out to Muslims and others who are far from God?

_____

_____

_____

_____

Turning Point: Another turning point in my life ...

What were some of the factors that led to this turning point?

_____

_____

_____

What are some of the ways life has changed for the better since facing this turning point?

_____

_____

_____

How can understanding this specific turning point in my life inspire me as I reach out to Muslims and others who are far from God?

_____

_____

_____

_____

Conversing in Meaningful Ways with Muslims

Over these first three sessions, Nabeel has given some insights and practical ideas on how to interact with Muslims in a way that is winsome as well as how to avoid unnecessary off-ramps in your conversations. Take time to think back over the lessons and identify some of the "dos" and "don'ts" of having rich and fruitful conversations with Muslims.

Some things to make sure I do when interacting with Muslim friends and neighbors:
⊕ Be gracious and talk about my own spiritual journey.
⊕ Know what I believe about my faith, the Bible, the cross, and the resurrection.
⊕ _____
⊕ _____
⊕ _____

Some things to avoid when having spiritual conversations with Muslim friends and neighbors:
⊘ Don't rely too heavily on the teachings of the apostle Paul but focus more on the Gospels.
⊘ Don't expect one conversation to change the heart and thinking of a Muslim … remember it will be a journey.
⊘ _____
⊘ _____
⊘ _____

Get to Know the Passion and Resurrection Narratives in the Gospels

Read the closing sections of the Gospels and write down everything you learn about the death of Jesus and His resurrection. Then, draw these insights together and reflect on what is central and core to the biblical account of these events.

Passage: **Matthew 26–28**

Insights about the death of Jesus: _____

_____

_____

_____

_____

Insights about the resurrection of Jesus: _____

_____

_____

_____

Passage: **Mark 14–16**
Insights about the death of Jesus: _____

_____

_____

_____

Insights about the resurrection of Jesus: _____

_____

_____

_____

Passage: **Luke 22–24**
Insights about the death of Jesus: _____

_____

_____

_____

Insights about the resurrection of Jesus: _____

_____

_____

_____

Passage: **John 18–21**
Insights about the death of Jesus: _____

_____

_____

_____

Insights about the resurrection of Jesus: _____

_____

_____

_____

Core lessons from all four Gospels about the death and resurrection of Jesus: _____

_____

_____

_____

_____

DEEPER LEARNING

As you reflect on what God has been teaching you through this session, consider reading Part 4 (chapters 24–27) of the book *Seeking Allah, Finding Jesus* by Nabeel Qureshi, if you have not done so already. In preparation for the next session, read Part 5 (chapters 28–31).

JOURNAL, REFLECTIONS, AND NOTES

JESUS: MORTAL MESSIAH OR DIVINE SON OF GOD?

If Jesus was the divine Son of God, we should

bow down and worship Him. If He was not,

then we should reject Him as a deceiver. The

words and life of Jesus draw a line, and we

must stand on one side or the other.

INTRODUCTION

SUGAR AND SALT look very similar. To the casual observer, they are almost identical. If you have ever gotten these two substances mixed up, you have discovered this truth. Just scoop two or three teaspoons of salt into your morning cup of coffee, stir it up, take your first sip—and you will know immediately that something is wrong. Sprinkle sugar liberally and accidentally on your freshly boiled corn on the cob, take a big bite—and you will know it with your first bite. Swap salt for sugar in your favorite cookie recipe, give a dozen of these homemade goodies to a friend—and they won't eat more than that first bite.

Salt and sugar might look similar, but they are worlds apart. The decisive moment is always the same … when we taste it! Our eyes might deceive us, but our taste buds scream the truth. Things that look similar can actually be dramatically different. It is not until we get past the surface and investigate further that we learn this truth.

To the casual observer, the idea that Jesus was a great prophet and the Messiah (the Muslim position) might look a lot like the belief that Jesus was and is the divine Son of God (the Christian belief). But if we take time to look closely and taste, we discover that these beliefs are as different as sugar and salt. What we believe about who Jesus is makes all the difference in the world.

If we can help Muslim friends, acquaintances, and neighbors dig a little deeper into the claims and life of Jesus, they might just see this difference. Most Muslims have strong convictions about who Jesus was (and is); they think their view is correct. But if we help them listen to the words of Jesus, see the actions of Jesus, discover what others say about Jesus, and really taste who Jesus is, they might just see the truth. Jesus is the divine Son of God.

TALK ABOUT IT

Describe a time when you mixed up sugar and salt, or ate some food or tasted a drink expecting one thing and got another. How did your taste buds tell you the truth?

or

Why is it important that we get past the casual first appearance of who Jesus is and really dig deeply into what He said about Himself? How has your understanding of

Jesus grown and deepened as you have dug deeper into the Bible and learned more about your Savior?

Every Christian should be confident that Jesus was Yahweh.
This is one of the earliest teachings of the Christian church.

Definitions

Blasphemy: The act or offense of speaking sacrilegiously about God; in particular, claiming to be God

A priori: That which is known through reason and independent of experience

Dualistic: The belief that the physical world and the spiritual world are radically different and separate

Hellenistic Jews: Jews in Jesus' day who were living in areas heavily influenced by Greek culture

Septuagint: The Greek version of the Old Testament, commonly used in Jesus' day

Muslims take extreme offense at the idea that Jesus ever claimed to be God.

VIDEO TEACHING NOTES

As you watch the video teaching segment for Session 4, use the following outline to record anything that stands out to you.

The biggest theological barrier for Muslims accepting the gospel

_____

_____

_____

_____

The Muslim challenge

• "Jesus never said he was God."

_____

_____

Why wouldn't Jesus use the words, "I am God" when claiming His divinity? Muslims often point out that Jesus never actually said, "I am God." They are correct. Jesus never declared His divinity with that specific statement, but He had a very good reason, and we should be ready to explain it to our Muslim friends. "I am God" is the way people today would expect Jesus to have introduced His divinity, but Jesus lived in the first century, not the twenty-first century. At that time in history the emperor called himself a god. Many times demons were considered gods. If Jesus had used that same language, it would have been confusing. We shouldn't superimpose upon Jesus our expectations for the words He would use. What we should do is take a look at what Jesus says in the Gospels about who He is. When we do so, we will discover that Jesus claimed things about Himself that belonged to God alone. Saying "I am God" would have been confusing. But by claiming the prerogatives of divinity and accepting worship, Jesus showed that He was indeed God.

- "Jesus says things that make it sound like he was not God."

- "God cannot and would not become a man."

God enters human history and comes into this world

When Christians talk about Jesus being God, and God entering into this world, this is not something new. Throughout the entire Old Testament we read that God walked with His

*people. God entering history is a consistent theme of the Old
and New Testaments, and we need to share this with Muslims.*

What the Gospels say about who Jesus was

• John _____

_____

• Matthew and Luke _____

_____

> *No one can read Matthew and Luke's gospels and conclude
> that Jesus is claiming to be a normal human. He is some-
> thing superhuman; He is something at the very least above the
> angels, close to God Himself.*

• Mark _____

_____

• A few thoughts about Paul's teaching on this topic

_____

_____

Discussing this evidence with Muslims

• Dealing with passages that could "seem" to indicate Jesus was not God

_____

_____

• Confidence as we study and search for answers with Muslims

_____

_____

The story is all about God, and this is beautiful

_____

_____

_____

What are the implications if a Muslim believes Jesus claimed to be God? Muslims insist that Jesus never claimed to be God. If Jesus did claim to be God, and if a Muslim concludes Jesus was God, then Islam is very, very wrong about Jesus and about Allah. Of course in Islam, Jesus is believed to be a prophet, and he could never have lied. He could never have sinned in most Muslims' eyes. So if Jesus claimed to be God (and claiming to be God is the greatest blasphemy in Islam), then everything they know about Islam is false. In fact, the Quran says that if you believe Jesus is God, your abode is hellfire.

VIDEO REFLECTIONS AND BIBLE STUDY

1. Why is our belief about who Jesus was (and is) such a central aspect of our Christian faith? Why is it essential that we understand and have the ability to articulate our beliefs about Jesus with people who do not share our deeply held convictions?

2. If you are talking with a dedicated Muslim who has studied Christianity, what arguments can you anticipate they might present to prove that Jesus was not the divine Son of God? How can you prepare to respond to these arguments?

3. Christians and Muslims have dramatically different views of God. For example, Muslims believe that God remains behind a veil and does not interact with people in any direct way. How is this different from the Christian belief about God?

And what are some biblical examples of how God has come through the veil and encountered people in both the Old and New Testaments?

_____

_____

_____

_____

How have you experienced God entering into your life and encountering you in a personal way?

_____

_____

_____

_____

Read: Isaiah 9:6–7 and Isaiah 7:14

4. Name some Old Testament prophecies that point to God entering human history at some time in the future. How can knowing these prophecies and talking about them with Muslims help them see that Jesus could have been God?

_____

_____

_____

_____

5. Muslims will often point out, correctly, that Jesus never said the words "I am God." They take this to mean that Jesus never overtly claimed to be divine. What are some reasons why it would not have made sense for Jesus to declare His divinity with these exact words?

_____

_____

_____

_____

How do Old Testament prophecies point to Jesus being God? Christians should be able to clearly present how the prophecies of the Old Testament point to Jesus as the one who would enter history as God with us. Isaiah chapters 7 and 9 teach that the Mighty God will be born, that the virgin will conceive and give birth to a child who will be called Immanuel. In Hebrew this name means "God with us." In the Old Testament, God comes repeatedly to His people, and then the prophets tell us that He will come again as the Counselor, the Mighty God, Everlasting Father, and the Prince of Peace. The New Testament does not say something new happened when God entered human history in Bethlehem's manger. It agrees with the Old Testament prophets and the recurring message of the Old Testament: God comes to His people.

Read: John 1:1–18

6. How does John use the language and images of his day to clearly teach that Jesus is divine? What does this passage say about who Jesus is, and how can this be helpful in our conversations with Muslims?

_____

_____

_____

7. Examine a few other passages in the gospel of John: chapters 5, 13, 14, 20, and 28. What does Jesus say about Himself or do here that clearly affirms that He believed He was divine? How could we share these accounts with Muslim friends to help them get a fuller picture of Jesus and His view of Himself?

_____

_____

_____

_____

All through the gospel of John we see Jesus saying things that only God can say.

Read: Matthew 26:59–68

8. The gospels of Matthew and Luke present a highly exalted view of Jesus. How does this particular passage in Matthew point to Him being divine?

_____

_____

_____

_____

> *Jesus said that people should honor Him the way they honor God. No Muslim would ever say that a human should be honored as God, yet Jesus in His own words clearly says this.*

Why do Muslims gravitate toward the gospel of Mark? We know that the Holy Spirit inspired every book of the Bible equally and that God's Word is true from beginning to end. But when we interact with Muslims, we are wise to focus on the parts of the Bible that they see as most authoritative. Mark's gospel is the earliest of the accounts of Jesus' life, and Muslims often see it as more authoritative because they think that the Gospels have been changed over time. Going to the oldest of the Gospels seems to connect most naturally with Muslims. A close study of Mark will strongly affirm that Jesus claimed to be God consistently and clearly when we read the gospel through a first-century lens.

Read: Mark 1:1–3; Mark 2:6–12; and Mark 2:23–28

9. How do these passages, and many others like them in Mark's gospel, build a strong case for Jesus being the divine Son of God?

_____

_____

_____

_____

10. Throughout the Gospels Jesus claims things, or has things ascribed to Him, that belong to God alone. What are some of the attributes or works of God that the Old Testament reserves for God alone but are placed on Jesus in the Gospels? How do each of these build a case for the divinity of Jesus?

_____

_____

_____

_____

> *The gospel of Mark presents it most clearly: Jesus is Yahweh.*
> *The challenge is we need to read this gospel through a Jewish*
> *lens. Once we do, the message becomes crystal clear.*

Read: Mark 14:53–65; Daniel 7:13–14; and Psalm 110:1

11. If you were a devout Jewish believer in the days of Jesus and you did not believe He was God, how would you have responded to the claims of Jesus in Mark 14? What does the response of the religious leaders teach us about what they believed Jesus was claiming? How does this passage build the case that Jesus believed He was divine?

_____

_____

_____

_____

12. In Daniel 7 we see a picture of two beings: one is the Ancient of Days (God) and the other is "one like a Son of man." When Jesus uses the title "Son of man" and points to this passage, what is He saying about Himself? How do these passages from Mark, Daniel, and Psalms come together to deepen our understanding and view of Jesus, and how can this truth be helpful in our conversations with Muslims?

_____

_____

_____

_____

Time and time again in Mark's gospel, Jesus is doing things that only Yahweh can do, things that the Old Testament says that Yahweh has the sole prerogative over.

13. If we are thoughtful and humble in our communication, how can we walk with Muslims through the Gospels to help them see that Jesus claimed to be God, that others believed He was God, and that the message of the Gospels is that Jesus was God with us?

_____

_____

_____

Why must Christians be able to articulate the fact that Jesus claimed to be God? Christians often take it for granted that Jesus claimed to be God without ever really having looked at the biblical texts that support this belief. This ends up being a problem in Muslim-Christian dialogue because when Muslims challenge Christians, Christians often simply do not know how to respond to the claim that Jesus really did claim to be God. It is really important, both for our own Christian faith and for the sake of Muslim-Christian conversation, to understand how Jesus claimed to be God.

When we read the four Gospels through the right cultural and contextual lens, the only rational conclusion we can come to is that Jesus was God.

CLOSING PRAYER

Take time to pray in any of the following directions:

- Praise Jesus as Messiah, Lord of the Universe, Son of man, Son of God, and the Divine One!

- Ask God to give you deep wisdom and a sharp mind as you articulate the reality that Jesus is divine in your conversations with Muslims.

- Pray for diligence in studying the Gospels so that you will know who Jesus is and how to share this truth with those who are still confused about who Jesus is.

- Cry out for God's power and presence in the lives of those Muslims who have come to recognize Jesus as the divine Son of God and who have followed Him as the Lord of their life. In most cases they will face family tensions, personal challenges, and often spiritual attack after making this commitment. Ask God to empower them.

> *Jesus told people He could and would answer their prayers.*
> *He promised that even when He was gone, He would be able*
> *to hear their prayers and respond. Since only God can hear*
> *and answer prayers, these words affirm that Jesus believed He*
> *was God.*

Session Four

BETWEEN SESSIONS

PERSONAL REFLECTION

Take time in personal reflection to think about the following questions. Journal your responses if you like.

How can you deepen your understanding of who Jesus is and what the Bible teaches about His divinity? What can you already articulate, and what do you need to learn with greater detail and conviction?

_____

_____

_____

_____

_____

_____

How did Jesus respond when others called Him God? In the gospel of John chapter 20, we find Thomas making a bold declaration. He had been in a crisis of faith and doubted that Jesus had risen from the dead.
(cont.)

When the risen Jesus appeared to Thomas, he bowed down on his face and declared, "My Lord and my God" (verse 28). Jesus' response was like saying, "Finally! Finally, you have understood! Blessed are those who haven't seen and believe." A good rabbi would have quickly corrected the disciple and said, "Never say that about me; I am just a man." There would have been immediate rebuke and correction. A Muslim likewise would expect Jesus to immediately refute Thomas' act of worship and declaration as blasphemy. But Jesus actually accepted worship as God.

What does the entire Bible teach about the person and work of Jesus? How should this truth influence what you believe, how you live, and how you tell others the truth about Jesus?

_____

_____

_____

_____

The Christian message, more than any other message, is about
God and what He has done for us.

Are you argumentative when you interact with non-believers, as if you are seeking to win a debate? Or, are you more gracious and humble, seeking to win the heart of a person to help him or her come to know and love Jesus? What can you do to grow in humble conviction and a gracious ability to articulate what the Bible teaches?

_____

_____

_____

_____

PERSONAL PRAYER JOURNEY

- Write prayers for specific people in your life who are not yet followers of Jesus (Muslims and others). Pray for their hearts and minds to be open. Ask God to give you opportunities and boldness to share the message of Jesus' divinity.

_____

_____

_____

_____

_____

_____

PERSONAL ACTIONS

Only God!

Over and over in Mark's gospel things are attributed to Jesus that belong to God alone. Only God created the heavens and earth, and only He has power over creation. But in Mark, Jesus is seen as Lord over creation again and again. Only God is Lord of the Ten Commandments since He gave them. Only God forgives sin. Only God deserves worship. Only God walks on water. Only God is the "I am." Yet in Mark, all of these are attributed to Jesus.

Read the entire gospel of Mark, identifying instances of something attributed to Jesus that is reserved for God alone. Use this list as a reminder when you share with Muslims.

Passage: _____

What is attributed to Jesus that is reserved for God alone?

_____

_____

What does this teach us about the nature and person of Jesus?

_____

_____

Passage: _____

What is attributed to Jesus that is reserved for God alone?

_____

_____

What does this teach us about the nature and person of Jesus?

_____

_____

Passage: _____

What is attributed to Jesus that is reserved for God alone?

_____

_____

What does this teach us about the nature and person of Jesus?

_____

_____

Passage: _____

What is attributed to Jesus that is reserved for God alone?

_____

_____

What does this teach us about the nature and person of Jesus?

_____

_____

Passage: _____

What is attributed to Jesus that is reserved for God alone?

_____

_____

What does this teach us about the nature and person of Jesus?

_____

_____

Passage: _____

What is attributed to Jesus that is reserved for God alone?

_____

_____

What does this teach us about the nature and person of Jesus?

_____

_____

Passage: _____

What is attributed to Jesus that is reserved for God alone?

_____

_____

What does this teach us about the nature and person of Jesus?

_____

_____

Passage: _____

What is attributed to Jesus that is reserved for God alone?

_____

_____

What does this teach us about the nature and person of Jesus?

_____

_____

Passage: _____

What is attributed to Jesus that is reserved for God alone?

_____

_____

What does this teach us about the nature and person of Jesus?

_____

_____

Passage: _____

What is attributed to Jesus that is reserved for God alone?

_____

_____

What does this teach us about the nature and person of Jesus?

_____

_____

Commit It to Memory

Some Bible passages are particularly powerful and helpful in a conversation with a Muslim. Of course, it is fine to keep a list of passages in your Bible or in your phone, but there are some poignant Scriptures that you can internalize through memorization and have ever ready in your mind and heart. Take time in the coming weeks to commit the following verses to memory.

Of course, memorizing the passages is only the beginning. You need to also understand the theological significance of each passage and be ready to articulate what each one teaches us about Jesus:

> "I am," said Jesus. "And you will see the Son of Man sitting at the right hand of the Mighty One and coming on the clouds of heaven." (Mark 14:62)

> In my vision at night I looked, and there before me was one like a son of man, coming with the clouds of heaven. He approached the Ancient of Days and was led into his presence. He was given authority, glory and sovereign power; all nations and peoples of every language worshiped him. His dominion is an everlasting dominion that will not pass away, and his kingdom is one that will never be destroyed. (Daniel 7:13–14)

> The LORD says to my lord: "Sit at my right hand until I make your enemies a footstool for your feet." (Psalm 110:1)

Jesus clearly communicated that He had authority to sit on the throne next to God and rule the universe with the Father. He claimed to be the Son of Man spoken of in the book of Daniel.

Prepared for Vigorous Conversation

Some conversation topics will come up often if you are talking about the Christian faith with a devoted Muslim. For example, a Muslim will say, "There are passages in the Bible (i.e., Matthew 24:36; Luke 2:52; John 4:6) that seem to indicate that Jesus was not God." It is wise to be prepared for these topics before you encounter them. Be ready to respond with a thoughtful and theologically sound answer.

How will you respond when someone points out that there were things Jesus said he did not know? (Matthew 24:36)

How will you respond when someone points out that Jesus grew in wisdom? (Luke 2:52)

How will you respond when someone points out that Jesus grew tired? (John 4:6)

In Jesus' day the only claim to blasphemy was if you uttered the divine name Yahweh or if you claimed to be God Himself (if you claimed the prerogatives of God).

DEEPER LEARNING

As you reflect on what God has been teaching you through this session, consider reading Part 5 (chapters 28–31) of the book *Seeking Allah, Finding Jesus* by Nabeel Qureshi, if you have not done so already. In preparation for the next session, read Part 6 (chapters 32–35).

JOURNAL, REFLECTIONS, AND NOTES

Session Five

THE CASE FOR THE GOSPEL

If Christians are going to share the gospel of
Jesus with Muslims, we must understand this
message and be able to articulate it in ways
that make sense to them. To do this we need
to identify the challenges most Muslims will
face when they hear the gospel, and we need
to be prepared to thoughtfully and graciously
help them overcome these challenges.

INTRODUCTION

IF YOU HAVE DRIVEN long enough, you have had an experience like this: Traffic is moving along nicely; you are on time; the sun is shining; the road is smooth; and the world is at peace. Then, for no apparent reason, you see brake lights ahead. Not just a few. As far as the eye can see, there are rows of red lights on the back of cars in front of you because traffic has stopped. Your car and day grind to a halt.

One hour and seven miles later you finish driving through the construction zone. Now the world does not seem to be at peace; you are running painfully late for an appointment; and the sun does not feel like it is gently shining but pounding down on you. You are behind schedule and, honestly, a bit frustrated!

Today we have access to apps and tools that identify construction zones and tell us where traffic is heavy so we can try to avoid such exasperating experiences. But, truth be known, there will always be times when we run into traffic, and the journey will slow down considerably. Knowing where the slow spots are can help, but part of driving is accepting the fact that there will be times when roads are blocked or bridges are out, when accidents happen or construction is unavoidable . . . and things will slow down.

As we travel down the road on our journey with Muslim friends and neighbors, we will also run into questions, conversations, and spiritual roadblocks that seem to slow things down. We should not be surprised or get frustrated. We should plan for them.

God is still at work, even if we see rows of red lights ahead and things seem to slow our journey of sharing Jesus. If we are patient and stay the course, we will move through the tougher seasons, and the road will eventually clear.

When we get to the point in our relationship and spiritual conversations where we can actually present the beautiful and life-changing gospel of Jesus, even this may present some potential roadblocks and detours. For Muslims, the idea of the Trinity and the radical grace of God can become a roadblock. We should be aware of this and expect it. With patience, humble conversation, and prayerful persistence, we can press through and continue on the journey toward Jesus with our Muslim friends.

> *The gospel message is this: God loves us despite our sins so much that He is willing to enter into this world, suffer alongside us, take our sins upon Himself, and die on the cross on our behalf. He rises from the dead so we can have faith in Him and our own resurrection.*

TALK ABOUT IT

Tell about a time you got stuck in traffic and ended up running considerably behind. How do you tend to respond in these moments?

or

Tell about a time you hit a roadblock in your journey of sharing faith with someone. How did you navigate this slowdown and press through?

> *The very three things that Paul says we need to believe in order to be saved are the exact three things that Islam denies about Jesus.*

Definitions

Trinity: The Christian doctrine that God is one in being and three in persons

Being: The quality or essence that makes something what it is

Person: The quality or essence that makes someone who he is

Elohim: Technically, this word means god or gods

Shahada: The central proclamation of Islam: "There is no god but Allah, and Muhammad is his messenger"

Shema: A biblical creed of Israel proclaimed by Jews twice a day: "Hear, O Israel: the LORD our God, the LORD is one" (Deuteronomy 6:4)

Echad: This word means one, but it often means two or more things coming together to make one

VIDEO TEACHING NOTES

As you watch the video teaching segment for Session 5, use the following outline to record anything that stands out to you.

What is the gospel?

_____

_____

_____

_____

The case for the gospel

What Islam teaches and believes about Jesus

> **What do Muslims believe, and not believe, about Jesus?** Muslims believe that Jesus is the Messiah. They believe that Jesus is virgin born, that He can cleanse lepers, raise the dead, and heal the blind. But Islam, very specifically, denies that Jesus died on the cross and that He is God. And if it denies those two, then it also denies the resurrection. The very three things the apostle Paul teaches that we need to believe in order to be saved are the exact three things Islam denies about Jesus.

Muslims will challenge the doctrine of the Trinity

• What the Quran says about the Trinity and what it does not say

> *The Quran clearly says that God is not three. "Say not three,"*
> *says the Quran. So, the Quran denies the Trinity. The real*
> *question is, what view of the Trinity is the Quran denying?*

• What the Bible says about God's plurality

- A response to the Muslim argument for simplicity

When Muslims are confronted with the truth of who Jesus is, they will often respond by challenging the reality of the Trinity or the extravagant grace of God taught in the Bible.

Muslims will challenge the radical grace in the Christian gospel

- How and why would God become a man?

- No person can pay for the sins of another person

- It is unjust for God to make Jesus pay for our sins

The message of the gospel is extremely gracious, and some of the parts of the Bible and Christian doctrine that don't make sense to Muslims are problematic because they do not see God as gracious at the core of His being.

Ideas for sharing with your Muslim friends

Don't try to convert someone as if you were the one doing the work in their heart. You're not. You're not converting them; you are witnessing to them. So be patient, prayerful, and ask God to work.

VIDEO REFLECTIONS AND BIBLE STUDY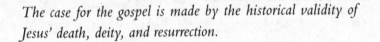

1. In Romans 10:9 we read: "If you declare with your mouth, 'Jesus is Lord,' and believe in your heart that God raised him from the dead, you will be saved." Nabeel points out that this one brief verse captures three components of salvation: (1) Jesus is God, (2) Jesus died on the cross, and (3) Jesus rose from the dead. Why is it necessary for a person to understand and embrace all three of these truths to become a Christian?

> *The case for the gospel is made by the historical validity of Jesus' death, deity, and resurrection.*

2. In your own words, what is the gospel? What does a person need to believe and confess if he or she is going to become a follower of Jesus Christ?

Read: Matthew 12:38–40

3. Nabeel talks about the "case for the gospel." In particular, he focuses on the resurrection as the moment when all of Jesus' claims were validated for the world to see. How is the resurrection of Jesus central to the Christian faith or, to put it another way, what would change about Christian faith without the resurrection?

4. What is the Quran talking about when it argues against "the Trinity"? What do Christians mean when we declare that we believe God is Trinity? How are we talking about two totally different things?

_____

_____

_____

_____

5. If you were having a conversation with a Muslim friend and they say, "I don't believe in the Trinity, so I could never become a Christian," how could you respond in a way that would clarify the meaning of the Trinity and help them take a step forward toward Jesus?

_____

_____

_____

_____

When God refers to Himself as "us" and "our," He is actually saying something about Himself. He is plural in some sense, yet his image is singular.

Read: Genesis 1:1, 26–27

6. What do the Matthew and Genesis passages teach us about God being one and yet also existing in multiple persons? How would you respond to someone saying, "The Trinity is a new doctrine invented by people in the New Testament era"?

_____

_____

_____

"What" He is, is one God. "Who" He is, is three persons ... Father, Son, and Spirit.

"Hear, O Israel: The LORD our God, the LORD is one." Nabeel explains that the Hebrew word for "one" in Deuteronomy 6:4 is *echad*. If we read this passage in English, it seems that the word is very clear. However, it is just as important to note that in the original language, the Hebrew word for a numeric one, *yachid*, is *not* used. The word *echad* refers most often in the Bible to a unified one. This passage speaks to the reality of the Trinity because it uses the word for a unified one (*echad*) and not the word for a numeric one (*yachid*).

Read: Genesis 2:24; Daniel 7:13–14; and Psalm 110:1

7. How do these passages support the idea of the Trinity being present and at work in the Old Testament? How might you explain these verses to a Muslim friend?

_____

_____

_____

_____

Why does the Quran deny the Trinity? Muslims are thinking of Allah when they say that God is not triune. The Quran very clearly says that God is not three. So the Quran denies the Trinity in that sense. What we need to understand and also learn to communicate to Muslims is that the Quran does not deny the Trinity that orthodox Christians believe in. The Quran denies a heretical Trinity. If you look at the Quran carefully, it envisions the Trinity as Allah, Jesus, and Mary. This is the Trinity the Quran denies.

8. Another possible roadblock in your conversations with Muslims is their resistance to God being complex and their sense that God should be seen as more simple. How does the complexity of life, the universe, and most of what we see move us toward an understanding of God that is more complex? How can a conversation about modern science, organic chemistry, or even quantum theory be helpful as

you talk with Muslims about the complexity of God and how this might impact our view of God as Trinity?

_____

_____

_____

_____

Is it fair to say God must be simple to be comprehended? Muslims are often concerned that a complex view of God is problematic, believing that God must be absolutely one. The reason Muslims think this is true is because it is what they have been taught … there should be simplicity to God. Here is the problem with such thinking: A simple God is not a God who would be reflective of the universe.

If you study atomic theory, you will learn that every physical thing is made up of atoms. These atoms are moving incomprehensibly fast. The electrons are circling the nucleus. When we look at a rock, a piece of wood, or a pair of pants, they do not look like they are moving. They seem to be inactive. But science has shown us that they are far more complex than they look. Things that seem inanimate to us can be active in complex ways.

If this is the case with the world God has made, how much more must it be the case with God Himself? If our minds can't comprehend God's creation, we should admit that we can't comprehend the Creator Himself. God must by necessity be more difficult to comprehend than His creation.

Read: John 14:28

9. How can a Christian say that the members of the Trinity are equal and divine, yet Jesus declared that the Father is greater than He? How would you explain this passage and declaration of Jesus to a Muslim?

_____

_____

_____

If the gospel is true, then Islam is wrong when it says that
Jesus did not die on the cross and did not claim to be God.

10. Because Muslims do not understand the Christian view of God's grace, it is hard for them to envision a God who leaves glory, becomes human, gets dirty, and gives His life for the people He created. How might Nabeel's story about a young Muslim woman saving her drowning daughter help the biblical teaching of grace come alive for our Muslim friends? What stories/illustrations have you found helpful to explain the radical grace of God? Share one of these with your group.

Read: 1 Peter 2:23–25; John 10:17–18; and 1 John 3:16

11. Muslims also have a hard time with the idea that someone else (Jesus) could pay for the sins of another person. Why is it important that we explain to Muslims that Jesus offered His life willingly? How can illustrations such as a parent cosigning for a house be helpful as we explain that Jesus took our burden on Himself? Share other Bible passages or illustrations that would help people make sense of the idea that Jesus willingly suffered and died on their behalf.

12. How does the cross of Jesus bring together both the perfect mercy of God and the unyielding justice of God? How would you explain or illustrate this theological reality to a Muslim friend or neighbor?

How does understanding the beautiful connection of God's mercy and justice impact your faith and the way you live on a daily basis?

How do God's mercy and justice work together? God is absolute and infinite. Muslims and Christians agree on this. Philosophically, this means that God must be the most merciful being in the universe — and, by definition, willing to forgive everyone. At the same time, God is infinitely just, and so must demand that every crime be paid for and every sin be punished. Herein lies the dilemma. How can God be both infinitely merciful and infinitely just at the same time? This is how he does it. He forgives every single person who accepts His penalty by paying the penalty for them. He Himself takes the punishment. The way God resolves the philosophical dilemma of His ultimate mercy and justice is by declaring the judgment and then paying the price Himself for all who will accept this gift.

CLOSING PRAYER

Take time to pray in any of the following directions:

- Praise Jesus for His sacrificial death on the cross and the glory of His resurrection.

- Thank God for the beauty and truth of the Trinity. Pray for the perfect community of the Godhead to be reflected in how you walk in peace and love with the people in your life.

- Give glory to God for being one in essence but three in persons.

- Celebrate the amazing grace of God and thank Him for leaving glory, coming to the brokenness of this world, and loving you personally.

- Thank God for the beautiful complexity of the created world, and ask the Holy Spirit to help you notice the beauty of all that God has made.

- Confess to God that you do not fully comprehend the greatness of His mercy and justice, but praise Him that they work together for your salvation.

- Pray for clarity of thought and boldness as you walk with your Muslim friends toward Jesus. Ask for patience so that you will not be discouraged or give up when you hit roadblocks along the way.

What is the case for the gospel? In a psychiatry ward it is not uncommon for someone to say, "I am god." This is called a delusion of grandeur. The fact of the matter is people claim to be God all the time. But if someone says, "I am God," and then offers to prove it by rising from the dead, they are offering to validate their claim by giving an objective means to test it. If first-century Jewish leaders decided to crucify Jesus because they understood Him to claim He was God, that makes complete sense in light of their view of blasphemy. But if Jesus said, "I am going to prove it to you by rising from the dead," then they had something to measure His claim against. Now we know, in light of history, that we have excellent reasons to believe that Jesus claimed to be God. We have solid reasons to believe He died on the cross and then rose from the dead. The case for the gospel is made by the historical validity of Jesus' death, deity, and resurrection.

Session Five

BETWEEN SESSIONS

PERSONAL REFLECTION

Take time in personal reflection to think about the following questions. Journal your responses if you like.

What are some of the roadblocks you are facing on your journey with Muslim friends or other people you are walking with as they learn about Jesus? How can you press on and get around these roadblocks?

_____

_____

_____

_____

_____

What new things have you learned about the truth and beauty of the Trinity in this session? How can you share these realities with others?

_____

_____

_____

_____

_____

> *The Trinity is one of the most beautiful doctrines in all of Christian theology.*

How do you see the mercy of God and the justice of God working together in partnership? Where do you still see these two great theological truths at odds with each other, and how can you grow in your understanding of how they work together?

_____

_____

_____

_____

> *How can God be both infinitely merciful and infinitely just at the same time? He forgives every single person who accepts His penalty by paying the penalty for them ... He Himself takes it. That's the only way God can resolve the dilemma, and He is completely just in doing so.*

PERSONAL PRAYER JOURNEY

- Write out a prayer asking for a deeper understanding of God's mercy and grace in your life. Also, ask God for such a deep understanding of grace that you can share it more naturally with others.

_____

_____

_____

_____

_____

_____

_____

_____

_____

_____

*God's majesty is important, and Muslims get that right. But
His love is greater.*

PERSONAL ACTIONS

Celebrating God's Complexity

Our universe is more complex than we know. From the very big things in deep space to the very small things operating on a subatomic level, the complexity of God's creation is staggering. During the coming week, take a fifteen-minute walk. Notice the beauty and complexity of God's creation. Write down some of what you see, reflecting on the immense complexity in a flower, a bug, a sunset, or another person. Then praise your complex God for His wonderful and complex universe.

What I noticed on my walk: _____

How is it complex? _____

_____

How is it wonderful? _____

_____

How does it teach me more about God? _____

_____

How can I praise God for this wonderful part of His creation? _____

_____

What I noticed on my walk: _____

How is it complex? _____

_____

How is it wonderful? _____

_____

How does it teach me more about God? _____

_____

How can I praise God for this wonderful part of His creation? _____

_____

What I noticed on my walk: _____

How is it complex? _____

_____

How is it wonderful? _____

_____

How does it teach me more about God? _____

_____

How can I praise God for this wonderful part of His creation? _____

_____

What I noticed on my walk: _____

How is it complex? _____

How is it wonderful? _____

How does it teach me more about God? _____

How can I praise God for this wonderful part of His creation? _____

_____

God must by necessity be more difficult to comprehend than His creation.

A Case for the Gospel

In this session Nabeel presented what he called "a case for the gospel." If we are going to have a positive impact on the lives of our Muslim friends, we need to be able to naturally articulate a case for the gospel in our own words. Below, write your personal case for the gospel, weaving in biblical passages, illustrations, and your own faith story. Keep it as simple as possible, but be sure to cover the basics of Jesus' story. My case for the gospel:

The gospel is absolutely beautiful. God loves us and is willing to sacrifice Himself on our behalf.

The Lord Is One

The *Shema* has been memorized by God's people throughout history and repeated as a reminder of who God is as well as who we are in Him. Before the next session, memorize this simple but powerful declaration, and say it as a prayer a couple of times each day:

> Hear, O Israel: The LORD our God, the LORD is one. (Deuteronomy 6:4)

> *The reason we yearn for love is that we are made in the image of the God who is love.*

DEEPER LEARNING

As you reflect on what God has been teaching you through this session, consider reading Part 6 (chapters 32–35) of the book *Seeking Allah, Finding Jesus* by Nabeel Qureshi, if you have not done so already. In preparation for the next session, read Part 7 (chapters 36–39).

JOURNAL, REFLECTIONS, AND NOTES

THE TRUTH ABOUT MUHAMMAD

To understand who Muhammad was we must
go back to the most ancient documents that
exist, and we must take them at their face
value. Integrity demands that both Christians
and Muslims draw their conclusions from the
best historical evidence.

INTRODUCTION

CURTIS IS IN LOVE. He met the girl of his dreams in his junior year of college; they have been dating for almost two years, and now he is ready to pop the question and ask for her hand in marriage. There is just one hurdle. He has to meet Susan's parents for the first time and ask them for their permission. He knows her family is quite traditional, and he wants to honor them. Because Curtis and Sue have been attending school on the East Coast and Sue's family lives in Oregon, until now they have only communicated by phone, text, and online—never in person. But now it's time.

After four days together, Curtis asks Sue's parents if he can have a private conversation with them. They are excited because they are fairly certain what he is going to ask. Curtis looks at them both and says, "I have a big question to ask you, but first I need to make a few observations." He looks at Sue's mom and says, "You don't keep a very clean house. I'm not trying to be judgmental, but I have to speak the truth. I am concerned with the example you have set for Sue."

An awkward silence lingers in the air, but Curtis does not seem to notice. He turns to Sue's dad and says, "I'm also concerned about how you interact with your daughter. You seem too close to her, and I think you're a bit controlling! I would suggest you give her a little space."

Then, to wrap up his expressions of concern, Curtis says, "I've also noticed that your dog, Muffin, is overweight. You feed and pamper her too much. She needs exercise and a healthier diet."

With a sigh of relief he leans back and says, "I'm so glad I got that off my chest!" Then, he asks the big question: "Well, I'm sure you saw this coming. I would love to have your blessing to ask Susan for her hand in marriage."

Wait! Who would be so dense as to drop these three conversational bombs right before asking his beloved's parents for the hand of their daughter in marriage? Obviously, very few people would behave in such a rude and insensitive fashion.

Sadly, when it comes to Christians interacting with Muslims, we can intentionally or unintentionally be rude and insulting and slam the door on our conversation and future friendship by the things we say.

These things can happen very easily when Christians say things about Muhammad if they don't have a close relationship with the Muslim to whom they are talking or a sensitive heart in how they communicate, or have an inaccurate understanding of Muhammad and how Muslims view him. If we are going to help a Muslim get a clearer picture of who Muhammad was as well as who Jesus is, we need to be sensitive, diplomatic, humble, patient, and prayerful. When we are, God can use us to shine the light of truth into some complicated and sensitive places.

TALK ABOUT IT

Tell about a time when you (or someone you know) compromised an evangelistic opportunity by being unaware of, or indifferent to, a social norm or theological sensitivity that mattered to the person you were seeking to reach with the gospel.

or

What are some things we might need to be aware of or sensitive to as we seek to share our faith with a person from a Muslim background?

> *Muslims believe that Muhammad is the greatest man who ever lived. Muslims think Muhammad was the best statesman, the best general, the best diplomat, the best father, the best husband, and the best at everything. It is fair to ask the question, does history support these bold claims?*

Definitions

Imam: A leader of Muslims, usually referring to one who leads prayer at a mosque

Mecca: The birthplace of Muhammad and the direction toward which Muslims pray

Medina: The city Muhammad fled to when he left Mecca

Monotheism: Belief in one God

Polytheism: Belief in many gods

Hadith: Authoritative traditions of Muhammad's words and actions recorded 200–250 years after Muhammad

Sirah: Biographies of Muhammad's life written 150 years after Muhammad died

Sunnah: Muhammad's ways of life, recorded in the hadith literature

Isnad: The chain of transmission for a particular hadith

Matrilineal: A culture or group where the inheritance or determination of descent is through the female line

VIDEO TEACHING NOTES

As you watch the video teaching segment for Session 6, use the following outline to record anything that stands out to you.

Muhammad's role in Islam

* How Muslims see Muhammad

* How Muslims see themselves in relationship to Muhammad

> *The stories of Muhammad's life are generally heard and learned orally for most Muslims. The large majority of Muslims have not gone to the primary texts about Muhammad and read them personally.*

The basic story of Muhammad's life

> *During his life, the Jews liked Muhammad because they were monotheist and so was Muhammad. The Arabs liked Muhammad because he was Arab.*

Sources that inform us about who Muhammad was, what he did, and what he taught

* The Quran

- Sirah

- Hadith

- Comparing the historical reliability of the Quran and the Gospels

An honest and historically accurate look at Muhammad

- Some good characteristics

- Bad and problematic characteristics and stories

The Islamic dilemma (facing the historical Muhammad)

Conversing with Muslims about Muhammad

- Talking about the real historical picture
- Talking about the reliability of the teaching on Muhammad's life
- Is Islam a religion of peace, and was Muhammad a man of peace?
- Discernment, wisdom, timing, and humility as we talk

Why is Muhammad so important to Islam? Muhammad is the symbol of Islamic pride and identity. When Muslims see Muhammad, they see themselves and their community encapsulated in one person. That is why they try to uphold his reputation and are so passionate about him. Not only is Muhammad important for the image of Islam, but he is also important for the theology of Islam. He is credited with being the conduit of Islamic revelation and the one who most exemplified Islam. What he did, how he lived, and his personal practices are the model for all Muslims. Muslims try to emulate Muhammad in even the smallest of things.

VIDEO REFLECTIONS AND BIBLE STUDY

1. Why is Muhammad so important to Islam and to Muslims? What could happen to the Muslim faith if serious historical examination were to show that Muhammad was not the person Muslims claim that he was?

   _____

   _____

   _____

   _____

Read: Proverbs 10:19; 11:12; 12:18; 16:23–24; 18:13, 21; 21:23; and 29:20

2. What do these proverbs teach us about the power and impact of our words? What lessons from Proverbs can you take with you into your conversations with Muslims, and how can these lessons help you share the message and love of Jesus more effectively?

   _____

   _____

   _____

   _____

3. Nabeel challenges us to enter conversations about Muhammad with caution, making sure we have a solid relationship with our Muslim friends before broaching the topic. Why is this so important? What kind of tone and attitude do we need to bring into conversations about who Muhammad really was and what history says about him?

_____

_____

_____

_____

4. As you look at the history of Muhammad's life, what strikes you? Why is it important for us to know Muhammad's story, both the good and bad, if we are to have meaningful conversations with our Muslim friends and neighbors?

_____

_____

_____

_____

5. Most Muslims are confident that the history of Muhammad they have been taught is accurate, though they have not studied the source documents themselves. If a Muslim actually were to read the sirah and hadith, what stories and teachings might surprise or shock them? How can you encourage the Muslims you interact with to read these writings on which their faith is built?

_____

_____

_____

_____

6. As a Christian, why is it important that you read the Gospels, study the life of Jesus for yourself, and not simply rely on what your pastor, parents, or Christian friends tell you? Why is it essential that we know what the Bible teaches if we are going to have meaningful conversations with Muslims?

_____

7. The Gospels were written by eyewitnesses and in the lifetimes of people who had walked with Jesus and heard Him teach. The foundational documents that shape the Muslim understanding of Muhammad were written about 150–250 years after the events they claim to record. What does this say about the reliability and historical integrity of what we can know about Jesus versus what we can know about Muhammad?

What is more historically reliable, the Bible or Islamic teaching? The writings about Muhammad's life were recorded long after his death. The sirah were written a century and a half later. The hadith, which are considered more authoritative to Muslims, were written more than two centuries after Muhammad's life. It is fair to compare them to the Bible as historical documents to see which are more reliable. People talk about Muhammad's life and Jesus' life as if we can be equally certain about what is recorded about them. The fact of the matter is we simply cannot.

The teachings of Jesus and the accounts of His life were written down by eyewitnesses and those who lived in the same generation. They were written at a time when many eyewitnesses were still living and could affirm or question the words of the Gospels. We can have a high degree of confidence, from a historical perspective, on the things written about Jesus in the four Gospels.

Such is not the case with the accounts of Muhammad's life, recorded so long after his death that no one was alive to corroborate facts and sayings or to refute a biased writer. Now to be fair, everyone is biased in some sense — the disciples of Jesus included. But the faith, identity, and lives of those who wrote the sirah and hadith were so heavily wrapped up in Islam and Muhammad that there is a high probability the stories were accidentally or intentionally altered according to the authors' beliefs.

8. As we interact with Muslims and eventually have conversations about Muhammad, what can you say about Muhammad that is positive and affirming? Conversely, what concerns about Muhammad could you raise, and how do you think your Muslim friends might respond to these concerns?

_____

_____

_____

_____

Read: Acts 17:22–31

9. In Acts 17, the apostle Paul was in a religious setting that could have been resistant or hostile to the message of Jesus. How did Paul approach these people, and what can you learn from the winsome and sensitive style with which Paul communicated?

_____

_____

_____

_____

10. Nabeel told a couple of troubling stories about Muhammad that are recorded in Islam's authoritative writings. How do you think your Muslim friends or neighbors would respond to these accounts of Muhammad's violence and approval of sexual slavery? In what setting might you be able to converse with a Muslim friend about these very serious accounts, and how would you approach these topics?

_____

_____

_____

_____

There are many things recorded in the historical sources that guide Islam that are very problematic and frankly, unconscionable at times. An honest person will face these and seek to make sense of them.

11. Describe the heart of the "Islamic dilemma" in light of what Nabeel taught in the video and the brief description below. How might you gently present this dilemma to Muslim friends? What are some ways they might respond?

_____

_____

_____

_____

_____

_____

What is the Islamic dilemma? Muslims who look at their faith with historical honesty run into a problem. One option is to admit that the sources of their beliefs about Muhammad are poor history written too far after the events to be historically reliable. This is no foundation for a real faith commitment. On the other hand, if they insist that these writings are reliable and paint a truthful picture of Muhammad, then they have to accept the many stories of violence, sex slavery, and human brutality. And if they accept all this, many Muslims will have to reject Muhammad as a prophet of God.

If a Muslim ignores or removes portions of the source material for their faith just because they don't like it, they are being arbitrary. They are creating a Muhammad they want and not the Muhammad history gives them. There is no way to cut one portion out and leave the other in. No razor can dissect between the good Muhammad and the bad Muhammad. You have to take them together.

12. It is very common to hear someone declare that Islam is a religion of peace. What does the history of Islam say about this declaration? What questions could you ask Muslim friends about Islam that would help them discover some of the true history of the faith they have embraced?

_____

_____

_____

_____

_____

13. Consider some steps Christians can take to help their Muslim friends continue on a journey of investigating the Christian faith and also scrutinizing their Islamic faith:

- How can we pray *for* our Muslim friends?

- How can we begin praying *with* them?

- What kind of study can we do together?

- What specific conversations can we have, and what topics would be good to address?

- How can we share more about our faith and the greatness of God's love and grace?

- What else can we do to continue our spiritual journey together?

_____

_____

_____

_____

_____

CLOSING PRAYER

Take time to pray in any of the following directions:

- Pray for sensitivity and wisdom as you talk with Muslims about challenging topics ... in particular, when you talk about Muhammad.

- Lift up prayers of confession and repentance for the times you have been insensitive in your interactions with Muslims and other people who are not followers of Jesus. Admit to God if there have been times you were more concerned with being right or winning a debate than loving people and seeing them draw closer to Jesus.

- Thank God that the Bible, His Word, is reliable, true, and has historical integrity.

- Pray for the Holy Spirit to open the hearts of your Muslim friends and neighbors and prepare them to hear truth, even if it shakes the foundations of their faith and world.

Session Six

BETWEEN SESSIONS

PERSONAL REFLECTION

Take time in personal reflection to think about the following questions. Journal your responses if you like.

How well do you follow the teaching of Proverbs to be slow to speak, humble with your words, and quick to bless and build others up? How can you grow in maturity and wisdom in how you use words?

_____

_____

_____

_____

_____

Where have you misspoken or behaved poorly in the past as you have interacted with non-believers of any persuasion? How can you learn from past mistakes so that you are more gracious and effective in your ministry of outreach to Muslims and others?

_____

_____

_____

_____

_____

_____

_____

How do you need to dig deeper into the Bible as you seek to share the gospel with Muslims and others? How can you dig deeper into the teachings and history of Islam so you can have meaningful conversations with Muslim neighbors and friends?

_____

_____

_____

_____

_____

_____

The earliest stories of Muhammad were written more than one hundred and forty years after he died. The Gospels were written between twenty to sixty years after Jesus' death. People who knew Jesus wrote them, and there were eyewitnesses to the events of Jesus' life still alive.

PERSONAL PRAYER JOURNEY

- Pray for diligence in study, boldness in sharing your faith, and humility in your interactions.

_____

_____

_____

_____

_____

_____

_____

_____

_____

_____

_____

PERSONAL ACTIONS

Practice Conversation

Take time to meet with a Christian friend and practice having a conversation about Muhammad as if you are talking with a Muslim friend. Seek to gently but clearly articulate your faith as you address a couple of these possible topics:

- The history and reliability of Islamic sources about Muhammad as well as the history and reliability of the accounts of Jesus in the Gospels

- The Islamic dilemma and how Muslims respond to it

- The accounts of Muhammad's violence and other troubling stories about him in the source materials that Muslims accept as authoritative

- Is Islam a religion of peace?

    After the conversation, have your friend give you feedback by answering the questions below:

  - Were you gentle in spirit and humble in your communication?
  - Did you ask questions and give time for them to interact and share their perspective?
  - Did you seem to know what you were talking about in terms of the Bible, Islam, and Muhammad?
  - What could you have done to communicate more effectively?
  - Were there any moments that felt like a conversational or relational off-ramp? How could you avoid these in the future?
  - How could you have communicated more effectively?

Once your friend has shared, switch places and have them try to articulate these same topics and invite the same evaluation.

> *We can know things about Jesus with a high degree of confidence. What we think we know about Muhammad's life can't be known with nearly as much confidence.*

Reading Original Sources

Take time to read some of the original sources and stories about Muhammad from the hadith. Become familiar with these and where to find them. An excellent website is sunnah.com, where you should probably explore the collection that most Muslims find trustworthy, *Sahih al-Bukhari*. The two books there that Nabeel has found most important are the books on "Fighting for the Cause of Allah (Jihaad)" and "Virtues of the Quran."

DEEPER LEARNING

As you reflect on what God has been teaching you through this session, consider reading Part 7 (chapters 36–39) of the book *Seeking Allah, Finding Jesus* by Nabeel Qureshi, if you have not done so already. In preparation for the next session, read Part 8 (chapters 40–43).

JOURNAL, REFLECTIONS, AND NOTES

THE HOLINESS
OF THE QURAN

The Quran is the "why" of Islam. If the
Quran is not what Muhammad and Muslims
claim it to be, the very foundation of Islam
crumbles and falls.

INTRODUCTION

SINCE 1985, PEOPLE have been enthralled with the world-of-boxing franchise of movies known simply as *Rocky*. Sylvester Stallone wrote and starred in all six of the *Rocky* movies and acted in the 2015 spin-off *Creed*. Each one has epic and dramatic fight scenes.

What Stallone learned over the years of making these movies is that the "knockout" is critical to the story. If you have seen any or all of these films, you might be able to close your eyes right now and picture Rocky falling to the mat—or Apollo Creed, or Clubber Lang, or Drago. You might even hear "Eye of the Tiger" or the *Rocky* theme song in the back of your mind as you remember these scenes. Though rounds pass and many flurries of punches are thrown, there comes a point when one punch lands and the fight is over.

When it comes to the Muslim faith, two pillars hold up the entire building. They are Muhammad and the Quran. If these two fall, Islam cannot stand as a viable and valid religion.

As Christians, we are not in a fight with people. We are called to be loving and gracious with the Muslims we meet. But we *are* in a fight for the truth. As we talk and walk with Muslim friends and neighbors, it is crucial to question their beliefs, the history of Islam, the person of Muhammad, and the veracity of the Quran.

If we discover that the Quran is not what it claims to be, not what Muhammad said it was, and not what Muslims claim it is today, this becomes a knockout punch for Islam. The Quran is not just a supplemental text for Muslims; it is the bedrock of their faith. It is eternal. It is everything to them.

With these things in mind, Christians should be humble but also bold as they talk with Muslim friends about the Quran. This conversation could lead to the end of their friends' Muslim faith but also the beginning of a new life of faith in Jesus, the one who brings true and lasting victory!

TALK ABOUT IT

What is it about the *Rocky* movies that has appealed to so many people for over four decades?

or

As Christians, our battle is not against people but against false teaching and a religious system that keeps them from truly knowing Jesus. How can we battle false ideas with rigor and persistence but still love our Muslim friends, family, and neighbors along the way?

Definitions

Inimitability: A doctrine which holds that the Quran has a miraculous quality, both in content and form, that no human speech or writing can match

Exegesis: The process of expounding or interpreting (particularly, Scripture)

Imam: A Muslim who has portions of the Quran memorized so that he can lead others in the five daily prayers

Hafiz: A man who has memorized the entire Quran

Doctrine of abrogation: The belief that some teachings and verses of the Quran have been repealed, usually by later Quranic revelations

Bucailleism: The technique of referring to the Quran for miraculously advanced scientific truths in order to defend its divine origin

Caliph: The leader of the Muslims seen as a successor of Muhammad

VIDEO TEACHING NOTES

As you watch the video teaching segment for Session 7, use the following outline to record anything that stands out to you.

The Quran is the why of Islam

* Muslims interact with the Quran very differently than Christians interact with the Bible

_____

_____

_____

_____

Five arguments used to defend the Quran as the word of God (overview)

- The "inimitability" of the Quran
- The "perfect preservation" of the Quran
- The "advanced scientific knowledge" found in the Quran
- The "accurate prophecies" in the Quran
- The "mathematical patterns" found in the Quran

_____

_____

_____

_____

> *The case for Islam rests on two things: Muhammad and the Quran. If a Muslim can show that Muhammad was a prophet of God or that the Quran is the word of God, then they have reason to believe in Islam.*

The "inimitability" of the Quran

- What Muslims believe

_____

_____

- This belief tested

_____

_____

- Logical and reasonable conclusions

_____

_____

> *We can't necessarily assume that just because something is the best there is, that it is therefore divine. This is not a good argument.*

The "perfect preservation" of the Quran

• What Muslims believe

_____

_____

• This belief tested

_____

_____

• Logical and reasonable conclusions

_____

_____

The "advanced scientific knowledge" found in the Quran

• What Muslims believe

_____

_____

• This belief tested

_____

_____

• Logical and reasonable conclusions

_____

_____

The "accurate prophecies" found in the Quran

• What Muslims believe

_____

_____

• This belief tested

_____

_____

• Logical and reasonable conclusions

_____

_____

The "mathematical patterns" found in the Quran

- What Muslims believe

_____

_____

- This belief tested

_____

_____

- Logical and reasonable conclusions

_____

_____

Do these arguments bear up under the weight of honest scrutiny?

_____

_____

_____

_____

How to speak with our Muslim friends about the Quran

_____

_____

_____

_____

*For the average Muslim, the Quran is extremely important.
The interaction that a Muslim has with the Quran comes from
the very first day of their life if they are a traditional Muslim.*

VIDEO REFLECTIONS AND BIBLE STUDY

1. Who introduced you to the Bible, and what are some of your first memories when it comes to the Bible? How do you interact with the Bible in the flow of a normal day as a follower of Jesus?

_____

_____

_____

_____

2. Very few Muslims read the Quran in the way Christians read the Bible for devotions. They don't interpret it personally or seek to apply it to their lives based on personal reading. Instead, they memorize portions to recite in daily prayers and for special occasions in life. How is this similar to the way some Christians and Christian traditions approach the Bible? How is this very different from the way many Christians approach the Bible?

_____

_____

_____

_____

Read: 2 Timothy 3:14–17 and 2 Peter 1:20–21

3. What do these passages teach us about how the writers of the Bible viewed the truth and authority of what is contained in the pages of the Old and New Testaments? Tell about how the teaching of the Bible has impacted your life.

_____

_____

_____

_____

How do Muslims approach the Quran differently than Christians approach the Bible? Muslims don't go to the Quran for devotions. That is a Christian thing. Christians will read their Bible and will do exegesis on it themselves. They will study it, interpret the text, and apply it to their lives. Muslims almost never use the Quran in these ways. They use it for liturgical purposes. They recite it during the five daily prayers. They use it to start an event by doing a recitation from it. The Quran has much more mystical value in Islam than the Bible has in Christianity. This is because Muslims believe the Quran is eternal.

4. The way the Bible came to Christians and the way the Quran came to Muslims were dramatically different. How are the Bible and the Quran different in the way they came into existence? Why is it important for us to know these differences as we interact with Muslims?

_____

_____

_____

_____

Muslims interact with the Quran regularly. It is part of the tapestry of their lives. They have tremendous respect for it because it is the why of their faith and not just the what.

How do Muslims see the Quran like Christians see Jesus? The Quran is not analogous to the Bible. It is actually analogous to the Christian concept of Jesus Himself. In Christianity Jesus is an eternal expression of Yahweh. Yahweh is one God with multiple persons, and Jesus is the person who is expressed in this world. In Islam there is one God, Allah, and the expression of Allah in this world is the Quran. According to the Quran itself, it existed in eternity past inscribed in heaven ... it is eternal.

5. Muslims argue that the Quran is the most excellent book ever written, thus proving that it is divine. Five times in the Quran we can read the claim that there is nothing else ever written that is as beautiful as the Quran itself. What are some of the problems with this as an argument for the divine nature of the Quran?

_____

_____

_____

_____

6. If you were having a robust conversation with a Muslim friend, how would you argue against the belief that the Quran is inimitable? Why does this defense of the divine nature of the Quran not hold up to honest scrutiny and basic logic?

_____

_____

_____

7. Another argument for the divine nature of the Quran you will hear is that it has been perfectly preserved over time with no changes in content or meaning or even the slightest change in punctuation. How does the very process that the Quran went through in being collected and finalized prove this claim as false? If the Quran were proven to be a human invention with mistakes, what impact would this have on a Muslim?

_____

_____

_____

> _Muslims claim the Quran is the eternally, unchanging, inscribed tablet in Allah's presence in heaven. In other words, it has always been the same. Therefore, if a Muslim discovers that the Quran has been changed over time, this becomes a major problem._

8. How does the history of the caliphs (the leaders of the Muslim people after Muhammad) and their debates and arguments over the content of the Quran stand in stark opposition to the claim that the Quran has never been changed? How does the intentional destruction of all of the earliest manuscripts of the Quran make it impossible to verify the claim that this book has never been changed?

_____

_____

_____

_____

The Islamic claim that the Quran has been perfectly preserved is not that the meaning has never changed. The Islamic claim is that not one letter or dash has changed. All evidence proves that this claim is simply not true.

9. How might you raise the historical concerns about changes in the Quran with your Muslim friends? What historical facts do you feel would be most helpful in this conversation, and how could you present these in a way your Muslim friends might listen to and possibly see the truth?

_____

_____

_____

_____

10. Muslims often claim that we can be sure of the Quran's divine origin because it contains advanced science that could never have been known in Muhammad's day. What are some problems with this claim, and how is the Quran actually inaccurate in its teaching about some aspects of science?

_____

_____

_____

_____

11. One claim for the divine nature of the Quran is that the prophecies it contains have been fulfilled. How could you approach this topic with a Muslim? What do they need to show you to prove this is actually the case? What would you have to show them to prove it is not the case?

Is there miraculous use of numbers in the Quran? Muslims claim the word for *day* shows up 365 times. They also say the word *month* shows up exactly twelve times. The fact that such patterns show up exactly the right number of times make Muslims think God must have been the author of the Quran. The problem is that neither of these claims is true. If you gently ask a Muslim friend to substantiate these claims, they can't. The difficulty is that the Arabic language can be fudged, and people can play with the data. But honest investigation demonstrates that the claim of special occurrences of numbers in the Quran is untrue.

12. Nabeel challenges us to ask our Muslim friends to explain their understanding of Islam more than seeking to prove them wrong. As a former Muslim, he advises us to ask good questions and let Muslims explain and defend their beliefs. For each of the five claims Muslims make to defend their belief that the Quran is divine and divinely inspired, come up with a question that would initiate meaningful conversation.

Question to begin a conversation about: the inimitability of the Quran

Question to begin a conversation about: the perfect preservation of the Quran

Question to begin a conversation about: science in the Quran

_____

_____

Question to begin a conversation about: prophecy in the Quran

_____

_____

Question to begin a conversation about: miraculous use of numbers in the Quran

_____

_____

13. Our concern should not be just the questions we ask or the discussion we have but also the tone and spirit we carry into these interactions. What negative or hurtful attitudes in ourselves should we beware of when we converse with Muslims? What positive and helpful attitudes should we develop instead?

_____

_____

_____

_____

> *Christians should show a lot of respect for and confidence in the Bible. Muslims do not generally think the Bible is reliable. But they have a lot of confidence in the Quran. The best response to the Quran is actually being confident in your biblical text.*

CLOSING PRAYER

Take time to pray in any of the following directions:

- Ask for humility and gentleness when you have conversations with Muslim friends about the very challenging topics of Muhammad and the Quran.

- Pray for opportunities to have rich interaction about these challenging topics, and ask the Spirit to give you boldness and wisdom in these discussions.

- Invite God to give you discipline and diligence in studying these topics in order to learn all you need for a well-informed conversation.

- Cry out to the Holy Spirit to prepare and soften the hearts of your Muslim friends so they can hear the truth and one day meet Jesus Christ face to face.

- Thank God for the Bible, and commit to grow in your love for Scripture and your discipline to read it and follow what it teaches for your life.

BETWEEN SESSIONS

PERSONAL REFLECTION

Take time in personal reflection to think about the following questions. Journal your responses if you like.

What do you really believe about the Bible, and what can you do to grow in your understanding of its truth and authority in the lives of Christians in general and in your life specifically?

_____

_____

_____

_____

_____

What do you desire and long for in the life of your Muslim friends? How do you hope that Jesus will impact their lives and transform them?

_____

_____

What steps can you take to go deeper in your relationships and spiritual conversations with your Muslim neighbors and friends? What is holding you back, and what will help you move forward?

PERSONAL PRAYER JOURNEY

- Confess where you have been fearful to have deeper conversations about the tough topics.

- Confess where you have sought to protect a relationship at the expense of speaking the truth in love.

- Commit to greater levels of humble boldness and deeper times of prayer for your Muslim friends.

PERSONAL ACTIONS

Building Confidence in the Bible

There are two best ways to build confidence in the Bible. First, read it every day. Open the Bible, pray for the leading of the Holy Spirit, learn from God's Word, and seek to apply what you learn to your life. If you have never read the entire Bible, consider following a one-year Bible reading plan and commit to keeping a journal as you go.

Second, study the history of the Bible. A solid understanding of the Bible's history will actually grow your confidence in its inspiration and authority. Consider reading *How We Got the Bible* by Neil Lightfoot for a basic understanding of the biblical text. An excellent book that will equip you to answer questions Muslims ask about the Bible is *The Gentle Answer* by Gordon Nickel.

Conversation Starters

Every person is different, and every relationship is dynamic. There is no one-size-fits-all program for entering spiritual conversations, which becomes even more of an issue when we enter into complex and emotionally charged conversations about the core issues of faith.

With this complexity in mind, write down potential questions you might ask a specific Muslim friend that will lead to conversation about the five reasons he or she believes in the Quran. Shape each question for the specific person and status of your relationship.

Friend: _____

Possible Questions:

Question to begin a conversation about: the inimitability of the Quran

_____

Question to begin a conversation about: the perfect preservation of the Quran

_____

Question to begin a conversation about: science in the Quran

_____

Question to begin a conversation about: prophecy in the Quran

_____

_____

Question to begin a conversation about: miraculous use of numbers in the Quran

_____

_____

Friend: _____

Possible Questions:

Question to begin a conversation about: the inimitability of the Quran

_____

_____

Question to begin a conversation about: the perfect preservation of the Quran

_____

_____

Question to begin a conversation about: science in the Quran

_____

_____

Question to begin a conversation about: prophecy in the Quran

_____

_____

Question to begin a conversation about: miraculous use of numbers in the Quran

_____

_____

DEEPER LEARNING

As you reflect on what God has been teaching you through this session, consider reading Part 8 (chapters 40–43) of the book *Seeking Allah, Finding Jesus* by Nabeel Qureshi, if you have not done so already. In preparation for the next session, read Parts 9 and 10 (chapters 44–53).

JOURNAL, REFLECTIONS, AND NOTES

Session Eight

REACHING YOUR MUSLIM NEIGHBOR

We can study Islam, understand what Muslims
believe, and know how to articulate our faith
with grace and passion, but this is not enough.
None of this makes a difference if we are
not in consistent and close relationships with
Muslims. If we are going to reach our Muslim
neighbors we must first build friendships that
are authentic and loving.

INTRODUCTION

Another Story of Three Friends and Three Conversions

IN THE FIRST SESSION of this study, we shared that the three writers of this guide, Nabeel, Kevin, and Sherry, have become good friends over the past few years. We shared that our conversion stories were dramatically different because we came from radically diverse backgrounds. Nabeel was raised as a devout Muslim; Kevin grew up as an intellectual agnostic; and Sherry was born into a loving and healthy Christian home.

Each of us traveled our own unique road to Jesus. But one thread was consistent in all of our journeys. God sent people to walk with us, love us, and show us the way of Jesus. They articulated the truth of the gospel, spoke of the love of God, and declared the message of Jesus' life, death, and resurrection. Through the love and witness of these people—and their passionate prayers that the Holy Spirit would show up and move in power—we each eventually came to place our faith in Jesus as the Savior and Lord of our lives.

For Nabeel, it was David, a college student. Together they spent four years talking, laughing, learning, debating theology, looking at history, and building an authentic friendship. For Kevin, it was two people. First, his sister Gretchen prayed for him, showed the love of Jesus, and invited him to places where he would hear the story of Jesus told in ways that made sense. It was also a college student a few years older than Kevin named Doug. This young man selflessly invited Kevin into his life and regularly shared stories of deep and personal faith in Jesus. For Sherry, it was her parents and a Sunday school teacher at her church. All three spoke patiently and gently into the heart of a young girl and lived lives of authentic faith.

In all of the complexity of life, when it comes right down to it, the most powerful things we can do are often the most simple. All of us can love, be a friend, share our journey of faith, serve, show hospitality, and tell the beautiful story of Jesus.

We should be compelled by the gospel in everything we do.

TALK ABOUT IT

Who did God place in your life to walk with you and help you come to a place where you were ready to enter a life-changing relationship with Jesus? What were some things this person did to help you along on your spiritual journey?

or

What is one step you need to take to move forward in a relationship you have with a Muslim friend or neighbor (or another person you know who is still not a follower of Jesus)?

Definitions

Marhaba: Hello or welcome, a secular greeting among Arabs

Assalamu Alaykum: Peace be upon you, the religious greeting for all Muslims

VIDEO TEACHING NOTES

As you watch the video teaching segment for Session 8, use the following outline to record anything that stands out to you.

The power of the gospel

- God's love

- The suffering of Jesus

- The hope of the resurrection

- The transforming power of the Holy Spirit

_____

_____

_____

_____

Sharing the gospel with people is giving them eternal life, or at least the opportunity to receive that message, and this is what should drive us.

We have the privilege of introducing people to their heavenly Father

_____

_____

_____

You might be the very first person to ever tell a Muslim that they are loved by God, their Father.

Natural ways to connect with Muslims

- Refugees
- Immigrants
- Students
- Muslims born in the United States
  - The place of prayer
  - Get out of your bubble and embrace discomfort

_____

_____

_____

If the only reason we spend time with a Muslim is to "get them saved," they can feel that. They will see themselves as an evangelism project. That is not how we ought to go about sharing the gospel. We should love them for their own sake and then share the gospel with them because that is the best way we can love them.

Ideas for building authentic relationships with Muslims

- Reach out like Jesus did (read the Gospels)
- Commit to walk with people for the long haul

- Be a friend for the sake of friendship

- Let people get close enough to you to see the gospel alive in your life

- Be transparent about your joys and struggles

- Seek to be humble at all times

- Know that you can disciple a person before they receive Jesus

_____

_____

_____

_____

> *Learn their language, be interested in their lifestyle, and become a part of their life. Let them into your life. Only by doing life with people can we truly show them our love for Christ.*

Some practical closing suggestions

- Warning: Be very careful about ministry between the sexes

- Practice hospitality
  - Be insistent
  - Ask good questions that show humility
  - Avoid showing pictures, pets, and the bottom of your feet
  - Be careful about food choices and alcohol
  - Serve tea
  - Learn language and lifestyle

- Know the place of prayer and the work of the Holy Spirit

- Tend to your own heart and spiritual life

_____

_____

_____

_____

Is your outreach organic or inorganic? If you sit down to meet with people and just talk about the gospel, and then you leave — and that is the only time you see them — it feels contrived, artificial to them. But if you have spiritual conversations in the context of everyday life, then your interaction becomes much more about understanding how other people think and how they see the world. Such conversations integrate into their minds naturally. We need to really do life together. We can invite people over to our homes, watch sports, share a meal, laugh together, and simply build a friendship. Friendship leads to organic outreach.

VIDEO REFLECTIONS AND BIBLE STUDY

1. What are some things that can get in the way of our engaging fully with people who are not yet followers of Jesus? What steps can we take to connect more meaningfully and consistently with the non-believing people God places in our lives?

_____

_____

_____

> *The reason we can love people, even to the point of death like Jesus did, is because we know that when this life ends, we are going to heaven. We have assurance of salvation. Muslims don't.*

Read: Isaiah 53:4–6; 1 Corinthians 15:3–4; and 1 Peter 2:22–25

2. If you were in a conversation with a Muslim and they were open to hearing you share what you believe about faith in Jesus, what would you tell them about:

• *God's love for you and for them?*

_____

_____

- *God's sacrifice and the cross?*

_____

_____

- *The reality and power of the resurrection?*

_____

_____

- *The hope of heaven and your assurance of salvation?*

_____

_____

- *Some other aspect of God's good news?*

_____

_____

_____

No message in the world can match the gospel for its beauty.

3. Nabeel explained that the Quran does not teach that God is a loving Father nor do Muslims believe this. What does it mean to you that God is your Father through faith in Jesus? How does this impact how you live your life? What would you tell Muslims about how God wants to enter their life and love them as a perfect heavenly Father?

_____

_____

_____

_____

Does the Quran teach that God is a loving Father? Many Muslims would say they believe Allah loves them like a father, but that is not actually what Islam teaches. It is definitely not in the Quran. As a matter of fact, the Quran specifically says in chapter 112, "Allah is not a father and Allah is not a son." Even more clearly in chapter 5, verse 18 Allah tells Christians and Jews that they are deluded for thinking that God is their father. They are just one of his creatures, and they should see themselves in that light. According to Islam, Allah is not the father of people.

Read: Luke 15:1–2; Mark 2:15–17; and Acts 10:23–29

4. Nabeel told the story of a young man who came to the United States as a student, bringing with him two suitcases of gifts to give to people who invited him into their homes. When he went home, he took the suitcases back with him, still full of gifts because he never received any invitations. What can we learn from the examples of Jesus and Peter about moving past fear and engaging with people whom others might avoid? Why do you think many people are nervous or afraid to invite a Muslim into their home or life?

_____

_____

_____

_____

   What can we do to overcome this fear and more effectively reach out to Muslims?

_____

_____

_____

_____

Far too many times I have seen people afraid to reach out with
the gospel because they are thinking, "What if I say some-

*thing wrong? Or, what if I make a mistake?" When it comes
to sharing the gospel, making a mistake or saying something
wrong is always better than doing nothing at all.*

5. Why is it critical that Christians be ready to walk with a Muslim friend over extensive periods of time rather than view the relationship as a quick effort to get someone converted? What are some consequences and dangers of seeing people as ministry projects and not as people deeply loved by God?

_____

_____

_____

_____

6. How can sharing our real joys and personal pain advance the spiritual journey we are on with Muslims friends? What can get in the way of sharing life on this deep level, and how can we press past these roadblocks?

_____

_____

_____

_____

*There are a lot of tectonic mental shifts that need to happen
in order for Muslims to see the truth of the gospel. So be ready
for the long haul.*

7. What do you think Nabeel means when he says, "Discipleship can begin before conversion"? How might a Christian begin to disciple a Muslim in Christian faith even before they have received Jesus as Savior?

_____

_____

_____

_____

8. In this study is a very serious warning about Christian men and women reaching out to Muslims of the opposite sex. Why should we take this warning seriously?

_____

_____

_____

_____

9. When we invite Muslims into our hearts and homes, two very different worlds are coming together. Discuss how you might implement some of Nabeel's suggestions in your relationships and interactions with Muslims:

- Be insistent about hospitality and offer food and acts of service more than once to break through cultural politeness.

- Be careful about exposing the bottoms of your feet or pointing them at people.

- Humbly ask if you are accidently doing anything offensive, and seek to avoid these things.

- Remove or be sensitive to having pictures of people around the house.

- Keep pets, and dogs in particular, out of the house or out of rooms where you will be spending time with Muslim friends.

- Be careful not to serve pork or food that might be pork-based, such as gelatin-based products.

- Don't serve or talk about alcohol.

_____

_____

_____

_____

It is when you actually live life together that the gospel begins to make sense to Muslims.

Read: Matthew 22:37–40

10. How does this passage, the Great Commandment, take on new meaning as you think about loving and serving the Muslims God brings into your life? What could it look like to love your neighbor as yourself as you deepen your relationships with Muslims?

_____

_____

_____

_____

Read: 1 Corinthians 3:5–9

11. What is the apostle Paul teaching us in this passage about our part and God's part in the work of evangelism?

_____

_____

_____

_____

Nabeel reminds us that we are not the ones converting our friends. Only the Holy Spirit can soften and change hearts. What part should prayer play as we walk on the journey toward Jesus with our Muslim friends? How can your group members be praying for you and with you?

_____

_____

_____

_____

Before you talk to your Muslim friends about Jesus, talk to Jesus about your Muslim friends.

12. As we minister to Muslims, one of the most important things we can do is pay attention to our own spiritual growth and take steps to strengthen our walk with Jesus. What are one or two ways you can do this in the coming months, and how can your group members support you in your personal spiritual growth?

_____

_____

_____

_____

CLOSING PRAYER

Take time to pray in any of the following directions:

- Thank God for His humility, for the cross, for His glorious resurrection, and for the wonder of the gospel.

- Ask God to bring Muslims into your life who can become friends and eventually family.

- Confess where you have kept Muslims at arm's length, or where you have seen them as a religious duty and project and not as people loved by God and you.

- Invite the Holy Spirit to grow your heart to be willing to experience discomfort as you get to know Muslims and invite them into your life.

- Pray for consistency in how you live your faith so that others will see what an authentic and passionate life of faith looks like.

IN THE COMING DAYS

PERSONAL REFLECTION

Take time in personal reflection to think about the following questions. Journal your responses if you like.

How has God humbled Himself to reach out to you? How can you humble yourself to reach out to people who are far from Jesus?

_____

_____

_____

_____

_____

How humble is God? God was willing to lower Himself. This is captivating because the Islamic god would never lower himself. But if it is good to be humble, shouldn't God be the most humble being in the universe? When we envision cultural heroes, we usually see them as radically self-sacrificing. Living a self-sacrificial life is a good thing, and reason says that God should be the most self-sacrificing being of all. According to the gospel, this is exactly who God is. He was and is willing to lower Himself. The Creator of the universe is willing to suffer at the hands of those He has created. That is powerful love!

How is God a loving Father in your life, and how can you help your Muslim friends experience this same intimate and powerful fatherly love of God in their lives?

_____

_____

_____

_____

_____

_____

> *When a Christian is given the opportunity to share the gospel*
> *with Muslims, we are given the extraordinary opportunity to*
> *introduce someone to their Father.*

In what ways can you open the door for more relationships with Muslims? As you begin to practice hospitality toward Muslims and invite them into your home, what are some things you will need to be sensitive to do or not do?

_____

_____

_____

_____

_____

_____

PERSONAL PRAYER JOURNEY

- Pray for the Holy Spirit to give you the courage to reach out and the humility to serve people well. Also, ask the Holy Spirit to work in the lives of your Muslim friends to begin opening their hearts to the love of their heavenly Father and a relationship with Jesus.

_____

_____

_____

_____

_____

_____

_____

_____

_____

PERSONAL ACTIONS

Getting Uncomfortable

In this session, you were challenged to "err on the side of discomfort." What are three or four ways you could do this? Write down some specific things that you know would stretch you and press you out of your comfort zone when it comes to reaching out to Muslims:

(1) Something that would stretch me and make me uncomfortable:

_____

_____

Why does this make me uncomfortable?

_____

_____

What step can I take to get past this?

_____

_____

(2) Something that would stretch me and make me uncomfortable:

_____

Why does this make me uncomfortable?

_____

What step can I take to get past this?

_____

(3) Something that would stretch me and make me uncomfortable:

_____

Why does this make me uncomfortable?

_____

What step can I take to get past this?

_____

(4) Something that would stretch me and make me uncomfortable:

_____

Why does this make me uncomfortable?

_____

What step can I take to get past this?

_____

Greetings

Take time to learn these two greetings:

- *Marhaba*: Hello or welcome
- *Assalamu Alaykum*: Peace be upon you

Ask your Muslim friends to help you learn to pronounce these correctly.

How can I learn great evangelism skills? The best evangelism training is reading the Gospels regularly and learning to do what Jesus did. Jesus reached out to people. He invited them to spend time with Him. He prayed with them. He discipled them even when they weren't yet believers. Jesus is the best evangelist, and we should try to emulate Him in our lives.

DEEPER LEARNING

As you reflect on what God has been teaching you through this session, consider reading Parts 9 and 10 (chapters 44–53) of the book *Seeking Allah, Finding Jesus* by Nabeel Qureshi, if you have not done so already.

JOURNAL, REFLECTIONS, AND NOTES

For many, many years we were sending approximately one missionary per million Muslims. I think God has finally said, "If you are not going to them, I will send them to you."

CLOSING WORDS

WE DO NOT HAVE IT IN OUR POWER to "convert" people from Islam to Christianity. This can only be done by the power of the Holy Spirit. What we get to do is introduce people to the gospel. We scatter seed. We can love, show hospitality, tell our story, explain the Christian faith, ask challenging questions, pray with passion, and respond to God's leading. We should see ourselves as a means for our Muslim friends to be exposed to the truth. We are witnesses for Christ, not prosecutors.

We anticipate and wait for the Holy Spirit to work. As we wait, we don't wait passively but actively. We pray to God, asking Him to work in people's hearts.

We must always remember that we are in a spiritual struggle that involves spiritual forces we don't always understand. The Bible tells us that our struggle is not an earthly one but one that exists in spiritual realms. With this in mind, Christians need to be extra attentive to their own spiritual health while ministering to Muslims. We need to expand our engagement in and commitment to personal spiritual disciplines. Fast, read Scripture, memorize Bible passages, and spend time alone with Jesus often.

Don't walk this journey alone. Talk about your ministry to Muslims with your Christian friends, and ask them to pray for you. Ask your church to pray. Stay connected in Christian fellowship. Grow in holiness. Run away from recurring sin in your life. Make sure you are strong in this time because Satan will seek to find a foothold in your life and cause you to stumble.

Finally, be joyful. God is working in you and through you for His glory. You have been given the privilege, the opportunity, to introduce someone to the heavenly Father they have never met. You are making an eternal difference. Rejoice, give God the glory, and press on. I am honored to be on the journey with you!

NABEEL QURESHI

SMALL GROUP LEADER HELPS

To ensure a successful small group experience, read the following information before beginning.

GROUP PREPARATION

Whether your small group has been meeting together for years or is gathering for the first time, be sure to designate a consistent time and place to work through the eight sessions. Once you establish the when and where of your times together, select a facilitator who will keep discussions on track and an eye on the clock. If you choose to rotate this responsibility, assign the sessions to their respective facilitators up front so that group members can prepare their thoughts and questions prior to the session they are responsible for leading. Follow the same assignment procedure should your group want to serve any snacks/beverages.

A NOTE TO FACILITATORS

As facilitator, you are responsible for honoring the agreed-upon timeframe of each meeting, for prompting helpful discussion among your group, and for keeping the dialogue equitable by drawing out quieter members and helping more talkative members to remember that others' insights are valued in your group.

You might find it helpful to preview each session's video teaching segment (they range from 25–30 minutes) and then scan the discussion questions and Bible passages that pertain to it, highlighting various questions that you want to be sure to cover during your group's meeting. Ask God in advance of your time together to guide your group's discussion, and then be sensitive to the direction He wishes to lead.

Urge participants to bring their study guide, pen, and a Bible to every gathering. Encourage them to consider buying a copy of the book *Seeking Allah, Finding Jesus* by Nabeel Qureshi to supplement this study.

SESSION FORMAT

Each session of the study guide includes the following group components:

- **"Introduction"**—an entrée to the session's topic, which may be read by a volunteer or summarized by the facilitator

- **"Talk About It"**—icebreaker questions that relate to the session topic and invite input from every group member (select one, or use both options if time permits)

- **"Video Teaching Notes"**—an outline of the session's video teaching segment for group members to follow along and take notes if they wish

- **"Video Reflections and Bible Study"**—video-related and Bible exploration questions that reinforce the session content and elicit personal input from every group member

- **"Closing Prayer"**—several prayer cues to guide group members in closing prayer

Additionally, in each session you will find a **"Between Sessions"** section (**"In the Coming Days"** for Session 8) that includes a personal reflection, suggestions for personal actions, a journaling opportunity, and recommended reading from the *Seeking Allah, Finding Jesus* book.

No God But One: Allah or Jesus?

A Former Muslim Investigates the Evidence for Islam and Christianity

Nabeel Qureshi

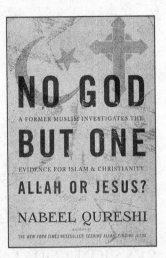

In *No God But One: Allah or Jesus?*, *New York Times* bestselling author Nabeel Qureshi takes readers on a global, historical, yet deeply personal journey to the heart of the world's two largest religions. He explores the claims that each faith makes upon believers' intellects and lives, critically examining the evidence in support of their distinctive beliefs.

Both religions teach that there is *No God But One*, but who deserves to be worshiped, Allah or Jesus?

Answering Jihad

A Better Way Forward

Nabeel Qureshi

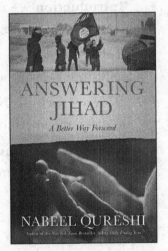

San Bernardino was the most lethal terror attack on American soil since 9/11, and it came on the heels of a coordinated assault on Paris. There is no question that innocents have been slaughtered in the name of Allah, and that jihad increasingly impinges upon our lives.

Setting aside speculation and competing voices, *Answering Jihad* provides insights to the questions we are all trying to answer. What really is jihad? Who are the true Muslims? Is Islam a "religion of peace"? And perhaps most importantly: how are we to move forward?

Available in stores and online!